If every just man that now pines with want
Had but a moderate and beseeming share
Of that which lewdly pampered luxury
Now heaps upon some few with vast excess,
Natures full blessings would be well dispensed
In unsuperfluous even proportion.

John Milton, 1608–1674

Ill fares the land, to hastening ills a prey,
Where wealth accumulates and men decay.

Oliver Goldsmith, 1728–1774

Beyond the Free Market

Rebuilding a just society in New Zealand

Foreword by the Rt Hon. Sir Edmund Thomas

Edited by David Cooke, Claire Hill,
Pat Baskett & Ruth Irwin

Dunmore Publishing

Published by
Dunmore Publishing Ltd
PO Box 28387
Auckland 1541
New Zealand
www.dunmore.co.nz

A catalogue record for this book is available from the National Library of New Zealand

ISBN: 978-1-927212-18-9

Text: Minion 11/14.6
Typesetting: Matthew Bartlett, Wellington
Printer: PrintStop, Wellington

The editors and publisher gratefully acknowledge the Council of Trade Unions and the Tertiary Education Union for supporting the publication of this book.

Contents

Note from the editors

One of the problems of talking about neoliberalism is the label itself. It doesn't mean much to many people, partly because the ideas of this particular form of economics have become firmly established as accepted practice throughout society.

These ideas are linked in New Zealand with 'Rogernomics', which means something to those with memories of the social and economic reforms of the Lange governments in the 1980s. Elsewhere, 'Reaganomics' and 'Thatcherism' ring bells for some.

In this book we use 'neoliberal' alongside, or in conjunction with, 'free-market' economics – in the full knowledge that the term 'free market' is consciously misleading and by no means sets out to create markets with open access. But it does have traction around the world and therefore offers a point of reference from which to launch a critique of the ideology that has driven New Zealand for the last three decades.

Foreword

E. W. Thomas

A remarkable editorial under the heading, "Thirty years after the revolution", appeared in *The Dominion Post* on Monday 14 July 2014. The "revolution" is the profound changes in the country's economy, foreign policy and race relations brought about by the Lange/Douglas Government in the mid-1980s. Some of the changes, the paper says, were for the better, but some were not. It is clear it considers the economic changes were very much for the worse.

The editorial is undoubtedly correct to remind us that it was nothing less than a revolution. In the subsequent two decades the welfare state and mixed economy were systematically dismantled and a deregulated free-market economy with the ability to dominate the political process was put in its place. The pure free-market creed that took hold changed the culture of our society from one where citizens with a sense of community pursued a collective purpose and accepted mutual responsibility for each other's wellbeing to one which worshipped the free market, ennobled the profit motive and gave rise to intemperate consumerism and materialism. The values of this acrid regime became the values of the community.

It is also right for *The Dominion Post* to remind us that it was a "Right-wing, top-down revolution which never figured in Labour's election manifesto". The revolution, it pointedly states, took place by "stealth."

It is sometimes said that radical economic reforms were required after the interventionist policies of the Muldoon era. But even if it is accepted that the Muldoon government's approach had created problems for the economy it does not follow that the reforms enacted had to be those embraced by the Far Right. *The Dominion Post* makes the point succinctly, "Douglas and his friends went well beyond sensible reforms and deep into the swamps of ideology."

The paper also records that Douglas said his revolution would put New Zealand on a new high-growth path, but bluntly adds: "It didn't". The "excuse" advanced for the failure of Rogernomics that the job was "left unfinished" is rejected as being something that only Act and the Tea Party could believe!

The economic theory underpinning the neoliberal revolution was never plausible and has now been comprehensively debunked both inside and outside the lecture room. The finance industry, it needs to be recalled, collapsed in 2008 because it had been deregulated in line with that theory. And indifference to economic inequality has proved socially and economically damaging and, notes *The Dominion Post*, is "now questioned even by the priests of the IMF and the World Bank."

Finally, the editorial states: "We are still wrestling with the legacy of David Lange and Roger Douglas." It is, of course, more than the legacy of those politicians. The neoliberal revolution continued under a National Government into the 1990s. The strong pursuit of free-market policies by the Minister of Finance, Ruth Richardson, is equally part of the history of the neoliberal revolution. The term "Ruthanasia" was coined as an analogue for "Rogernomics". This book verifies the many respects in our social, political and economic life in which we are still "wrestling with the legacy" of that time.

But the economic changes are to be perceived, not only as a revolution, but also as a regression. Based on extensive research and data dating back beyond the industrial revolution, Thomas Piketty, in *Capital in the Twenty-First Century* (Harvard, 2014), concluded that capitalist societies today exhibit "an arbitrary and inequitable distribution of wealth and income". Among his many insights is the finding that the rate of return on capital tends to exceed the rate of economic growth. A finding that the return on capital is greater than the return on labour necessarily means that, unless checked, ever increasing inequality is inherent in capitalism. Added to this factor is Piketty's description of "patrimonial capitalism" whereby inherited wealth has become a major factor in amassing the fortunes of the rich. Arrested by the emergence of the welfare state and mixed economy after World War II, the neoliberal revolution enabled this inherent trend in capitalism to reassert itself. It caused society to regress to a form of capitalism that had been experienced, found wanting and rejected by society.

In this context, the introduction of neoliberal economics by the Labour Government was nothing short of political treachery. Not only was the Far Right economic regime instituted by a Labour Government, but also it was instituted without any electoral forewarning and without any show of public consultation. But it was not just a political betrayal. It was the betrayal of the traditional values of the Labour Party. As to be expected, the values of that Party had developed since the days of Harry Holland and Michael Joseph Savage, but the values had never remotely embraced the values of an unfettered free market carrying individual responsibility to an unrealistic extreme. In betraying the values of the Labour Party, Rogernomics also betrayed the trust of its members and supporters, a betrayal made more acute by the speed and "stealth" of its delivery.

The fact that the Labour Party was hijacked by Rogernomics also meant that this country was deprived of a major political voice advocating values contrary to that ideology. If the neoliberal economics had been instituted by a party on the Right, the Labour Party could have been expected to oppose that creed and expose the mantras and myths on which it is based. It could, for example, have countered the surge towards deregulation by reiterating that responsible regulation is the means by which citizens in a democratic society are able to ensure that the free market works for the public good, or it could have refuted the premise that lower taxes on the rich leads to greater economic growth, or it could have otherwise refuted any of the other mantras and myths which are peddled by the rich and powerful to secure their wealth and privilege. But this voice for a more rational economy based on collective and inclusive values and a sense of community was absent. How could it be otherwise when the Party promoting and implementing this pure free-market regime was the Labour Party itself? The voice that could have been expected to speak out against the dismantling of the values of a social democracy and the importation of the values of neoliberalism was the very voice promoting that regime.

The ills which persist are set out in the chapters of this book with clarity and force. Space prevents me from referring to each chapter in turn. What I propose to do, without trespassing on the authors' contributions, is to briefly touch upon some points relating to labour relations, health, education and welfare.

The effect of the neoliberal revolution on working people has been devastating and savage. Arbitration, compulsory unionism, and the award system of bargaining with employers were swept away. Collective bargaining was shelved in favour of individual contracts between employer and employee. Successive governments have whittled away the workers' rights and traduced their contribution to the economy and to society as a whole. The power of trade unions, which is to say the collective voice of workers, has been decimated. Wages have stagnated and working conditions have become increasingly harsh. Profits have been put ahead of safety.

Moreover, workers have been required to bear many of the risks inherent in the operation of the free market without the prospect of a financial return for bearing the risks. The potential failure of a business, for example, is shifted to the worker by way of a risk that he or she will be made redundant or that their wages will be depressed and not keep pace with the cost of living. The risk that the worker will suffer an incapacitating accident, or even death, as a result of inadequate safety controls neglected in the pursuit of profit is another example. It is because workers bear these risks that they should be regarded as stakeholders in the industry to which they provide their labour.

The individual employee is no match for the employer. Historically, the only way in which workers could resist becoming a commodity and subject to the drive to secure profit was to bargain as a group. As part of the neoliberal economic surge they have been denied that freedom. To the contrary, they have been encouraged to believe that their true freedom is the freedom to belong or not to belong to any association, in this case, a trade union. Workers may have achieved this simulated freedom of association but they have lost their economic freedom. The worker has come to be regarded as a commodity or unit of production and, in the result, is denied the human dignity which is the right of every human being.

Health has suffered from the misguided belief that free-market theory can be applied to health care. But illnesses fall most heavily on groups that are marginalised or come from poor environments. The statistics relating to Māori are particularly appalling; Māori life expectancy is eight years lower than Pākehā life expectancy; Māori have a 50 per cent higher rate of mental illness than non-Māori; and Māori children are much more prone to certain illnesses, such as rheumatic fever.

The extent to which our rivers and lakes are being polluted to the detriment of our health deserves attention. What is happening is the privatisation of water. Water, which belongs to all the people, is being appropriated for private profit and then, to compound the evil, is returned to the people in a drastically polluted condition. It is a problem which the market cannot resolve. Decisive government action is required, but the measures so far introduced fall far short of meeting the problem. A *laissez faire* indifference, rejuvenated under neoliberalism, has resulted in our waterways being polluted and future generations burdened with an unwanted ecological debt. The Government's approach also perpetuates the myth that it is necessary to choose between economic growth and the protection of the environment, when we can have both.

Nor has education escaped the free-market scythe. Indeed, it has been mutated from an essentially collective funded public good into a private good at considerable cost to both students and the community.

One early indication symptomatic of the free-market approach to education was the Government's axing of adult and community education programmes. Spending on such programmes is wrongly perceived to be "low value spending". But more than that, cutting the adult education programmes adrift shows a lack of empathy for those who seek to take advantage of them. Such programmes not only provided individuals with the opportunity to advance their capabilities and skills but also did much to bolster their self-esteem. The growth in their self-respect was matched by the growth in the contribution they could make to the community. But of course, empathy for these hopeful latecomers, as in other aspects where the free-market economics has taken its toll, is in short supply. Empathy in a free-market economy is a scarce resource.

Behind the market-driven approach to education is the Right's seemingly intractable mistrust and hostility towards teachers. The Right seem congenitally unable to treat teachers as responsible and dedicated professionals fully alert to the educational and wider needs of the young. They exhibit little, if any, appreciation that teaching is a vocation and adhere to a warped view that the quality of teaching can only be improved by the provision of monetary incentives.

Furthermore, it is as if the Right is seeking to hold teachers responsible for the ills of society. Yet, it is beyond argument that the "outcomes" achieved by schools reflect the socio-economic status of the school's catchment area and the social and economic health of the immediate community. If children are underachieving, it seems, it is much easier for the Right to blame the teachers rather than admit that the problem is the socio-economic deficiencies that are the responsibility of government.

The growing disparity in educational opportunity is a major cause for concern. Under the mantra of providing "choice", private schools have been politically endowed with liberal state funding. This development has occurred at the expense of our once cherished system of public education. The "choice", of course, is again the province of the wealthier members of our society. Inequality in educational opportunity has in turn led to greater economic inequality and had a seriously adverse effect on social mobility.

The welfare system has also suffered the ravages of free-market thinking. Low benefit levels, low wages and continuing unemployment are now the norm. The attitude to beneficiaries by many in the community is particularly distressing. The great majority of beneficiaries are honest people striving to make the best of their lot. Yet, the image of them fabricated by the Right portrays them as "welfare cheats" or "bludgers". At times there is a subtle inference that they are indulging in excessive smoking, drinking and gambling at the expense of the taxpayer. As any social worker will confirm, this depiction is grossly inaccurate and unfair. Manufactured stereotyping of beneficiaries in this way is particularly galling when regard is had to the fact that tax avoidance, which is a not uncommon business practice, costs the country many more millions of dollars than welfare fraud.

At root, what is at issue is a question of values. Is the community content to continue to endorse the values generated by the free market or will it aspire to the collective values inherent in a welfare state and social democracy? My concern is that free-market ideology with its plethora of mantras and myths has captured the battleground. A culture of liberal individualism has taken hold. It seems that something approaching a revolution in thought will be necessary to lay the foundation for a more inclusive, equal and fair society. But if that is what is required, good men and women of whatever political persuasion must work to bring about this revolution in thinking.

Such good men and women exist. Our country is full of people who are optimists, altruists, idealists and other like-minded people who care, people who are empathetic, people who are not satisfied with the way things are, people who will not despair, and people who will strive to achieve a fairer world and improve the lot of humankind. People are fully capable of empathy, as witness the response to natural disasters such as the Christchurch earthquake. The empathy, however, is the empathy of the individual, not the collective empathy of a socially responsible community. Restoring or converting this capacity for empathy to the body politic is probably the most difficult task facing the post-neoliberal reconstruction.

The chapters in this book point to the respects in which the values of the free market must be rejected. Certainly, capitalism is capable of adjustment. Universal franchise, the growth of a propertied middle class and the emergence of the welfare state are notable manifestations of this capacity. In short, the economic order must be adjusted and replaced by the more inclusive, equal and fair society heralded in this book.

A number of themes spring out from the various chapters with disturbing regularity:

- a blind, ideological faith in free-market economics and a steadfast refusal to admit that pure free-market theory is flawed;
- a readiness to perpetuate the mantras and myths necessary to sustain the wealth and privilege of the rich and powerful;

- an undue preparedness to rely on evidence favourable to free-market ideology and ignore or misrepresent evidence that is not;
- a resolute determination to promote the concept of individual responsibility as an absolute value, a concept which is both unrealistic and socially effete;
- a propensity to believe that misfortunes, more often than not due to the economy, such as unemployment, financial hardship, poverty, and even ill health, are somehow a person's own fault;
- a failure to perceive that government intervention in the economy is the means by which citizens in a democracy harness the free market so that it works for the public good;
- an inability in assessing any issue to see beyond the immediate circumstances and have regard to externalities, indirect or hidden costs, intangible values and the potential burden on future generations;
- a dismal perception of the public good and of concepts such as altruism, inclusiveness, collective responsibility, a mutual responsibility for others' wellbeing, and a sense of community;
- a failure to appreciate that the free market is a difficult place for the insecure and frangible and that not all people who make up our society are equipped to succeed in that market;
- a readiness to regard large groups of people, workers, students and other sectors serving the public weal, as fodder for the operation of the free-market economy;
- a belligerent dismissal of the fact a free-market economy has no inbuilt mechanism to protect the environment or sustain our natural resources;
- a lack of genuine empathy for the plight of the underprivileged, disadvantaged and marginalised in our society; and
- a bereft vision of people's humanity and a profound inability to comprehend the inherent dignity which is the right of all human beings.

The same chapters make it clear, however, that we can do better. New Zealanders have not forgotten their proud history of egalitarianism, social justice and fair play. They have come to appreciate that the neoliberal revolution was an appalling mistake and that our society is all the worse for it. This book will have served a valuable purpose if it reinforces our society's sense of equality, social justice and fair play and leads, with perhaps a hesitant step or two, to the eradication of the legacy of neoliberalism and the building, or rebuilding, of a society dedicated to the values of a fair society.

Setting the Scene

The Political Restructuring of New Zealand

Nicky Hager

Nineteen ninety-three was the date when the majority of New Zealanders turned against the free-market policies of Roger Douglas and Ruth Richardson. The National Government nearly lost an election that year and dropped Richardson as Minister of Finance. The Labour Party simultaneously dumped its free-market leader Mike Moore for Helen Clark. And the public, sick of abuses of government power, voted to adopt the MMP proportional voting system.

After nine years of privatisation, deregulation and cutting public services, opinion had swung decisively against free-market policies. Yet more than 20 years after that profound change in public opinion, New Zealand still retains many of the policies of the 1980s and early 1990s. Why?

I believe this is the most important question facing New Zealand politics, far more so than personalities, polls and party problems. Why didn't New Zealand move back to a mainstream position in economic and social policy in the generation since Rogernomics? Why do we still have a suite of policies that create ever greater inequality? Why do left-wing politicians seem unable to change many policies? And why do politicians on the right seem to have few ideas to address the nation's needs and problems beyond more privatisation and deregulation?

The answer to these questions lies in changes to the political environment that occurred during the free-market years. There are three parts to this political restructuring. First, there has been a dramatic growth in the political influence of free-market and business lobbies. Second, there's been a decline in public interest groups and institutions. Third, this shift in power from public to business groups has unhappily coincided with other changes occurring worldwide: the decline of news media, the growth of public relations, and professionalisation of political lobbying, each of which acts to reduce the influence of the public in politics compared to business.

These changes have direct effects on politics. Take, for instance, climate change. The 1999–2008 Labour Government's main policy initiative on climate change was the attempt to introduce a carbon tax in the early 2000s. But it hit a wall of opposition. A London School of Economics study found that well over 90% of news coverage on the proposed tax was negative. Faced with this apparent outpouring of opposition, Labour eventually dropped its plans. The LSE study, however, discovered that the anti-carbon tax news had largely been orchestrated by a Wellington firm of PR people and lobbyists. Their client, whose role was kept secret throughout, was the New Zealand coal industry. The journalists covering the issue never realised what was going on and public interest groups were unaware of the source of the overwhelming campaign against them.

It is the same whenever economic policies are proposed that would undo some of the free-market reforms and/or affect an influential sector's profits. The typical response is a barrage of public criticism or quiet pressure to discourage the politicians from that course. In April 2013, for instance, the Labour and Green parties announced a joint policy aimed at reducing electricity prices. They proposed a single-buyer organisation called New Zealand Power to negotiate lower rates for the public and businesses. There was a wave of angry and extravagant criticism. The plan was "mad Soviet-style policy", "Albanian", "North Korean", "crazy", "wacky", "loony tunes", "absurd", "vandalism", "Stalinism", a return to "United Soviet Socialist Republic of New Zealand days" and so on; the opposite of rational debate.

A single government electricity buyer is seen as sensible, mainstream policy in other countries, but the insults imply that anything but free-market policies are unthinkable. The aim is to create a political environment where policy change is difficult or impossible.

Besides politicians and their blogging allies, these comments came from an array of industry commentators. A constant presence in the news of paid spokespeople from finance, investment and business organisations is an important part of the political realignment that accompanied the free-market reforms.

Also, several of the attacks on the policy proposal came from media personalities, three of them prominent in the Newstalk ZB radio network. The nationwide network of Newstalk ZB stations used to be part of Radio New Zealand until they were privatised in 1996. Today Newstalk ZB is 50% owned by a conservative US radio network and, like other private local radio, outwardly populist, but most often aligned to the right of politics. The Newstalk

ZB media personalities repeated the arguments coming from industry lobby groups and declared the Labour-Green electricity policy to be "economic sabotage", "Muldoon price fixing" and a "big mistake [that] can't work".

All of this matters greatly in politics. If a policy is announced and most people appear to oppose it, it will be much harder for politicians to introduce it. Or if controversial policy is announced but many people appear to support it, it is more likely to be implemented. However, 'most people' often does not mean a majority of the public. It can simply mean the voices that are heard most often and loudly.

This process creates the political environment, as stories like the carbon tax and electricity reform are repeated issue by issue, year after year. The paid industry lobbying is a big part of why it has been so difficult for New Zealand to move on from the free-market era.

Here is a list of some of the tools available for this corporate political activism:

- PR companies specialising in media campaigns and other sophisticated campaigning to win public and government support for their clients' interests;
- specialist lobby firms to work for and against government policy according to their clients' preferences, often on issues the public doesn't even hear about;
- specialist 'government relations' staff in law firms using legal tools to influence government decisions;
- political intelligence services;
- specialist opinion surveying and research organisations to assist political campaigns;
- for-hire services to monitor and try to minimise the impact of their clients' public opponents;
- paid spokespeople to join in 'public' debate.

Many types of business, especially controversial ones, fund spokespeople to speak in the news media on issues affecting their employers. Commercialised news media with skeleton staffs are happy to use these on-call experts and so they are sitting ducks for well-resourced PR campaigns. The decline of news media has assisted the growth of paid manipulators.

In all these ways, industry lobby groups can simply spend money and have a large and continuous impact on politics. Where helpful, they can do this at arms-length, for instance putting money into apparently spontaneous public campaigns fronted by PR people and funded from undisclosed sources. Notable recent examples in New Zealand are anti-MMP campaigns, campaigns against tobacco regulations and a campaign to fight election donation laws (election donations are of course another tool for buying influence).

The availability of political tools for hire has grown at the same time as the free-market policies have concentrated wealth (and thus the ability to buy political influence) in fewer hands. The groups who benefited from deregulation have a strong motivation to resist change.

One of the crucial strategies for maintaining free-market policy involves the language used in political debate. Note the extreme language used against a middle-of-the-road piece of social policy like the Labour-Green electricity plan. For 30 years, whenever a government has considered regulating the economy in the public good – or indeed considered almost any policy that is not the purest 1980s and 1990s free market – it has been attacked as socialist, fringe and (a potent phrase imported from overseas right-wing parties) a Nanny State.

This language has been very influential in suppressing change and neatly fits the definition of propaganda, meaning language of persuasion based on deception. For it is just not true. Prior to the free-market years, New Zealand was a moderate, private enterprise, social welfare state. Since then, it has the sad distinction of being at the far-right extreme of deregulated, free-market countries.

This is seen in the Economic Freedom Index ranking of countries done each year by a right-wing US lobby group called the Heritage Foundation. It ranks countries by their financial, investment, labour and business 'freedoms': meaning their lack of labour protections, lack of constraints on banks to maximise profits, lack of controls on foreign companies and so on. For most of the past 20 years, Hong Kong and Singapore have come first and second out of 177 countries in the business-friendly stakes, and New Zealand has been third. In 2013 it is sitting at fourth.

This is very far from being a Nanny State and also very far from what most New Zealanders imagine or want for their country. The ranking explains why New Zealand has such rapidly growing disparity between rich and poor people. Inequality is the inevitable price of a deregulated and privatised society. But the nanny-state language has served to hide the reality, confuse public discussion and dampen calls for change.

There is another important factor that explains the political environment. Throughout the 1980s and 1990s it was a career-enhancing move for politicians, public servants, academics, media people, business people, people in organisations such as Federated Farmers and so on to repeat the free-market mantra against regulations, tax and public spending. These people were promoted to high levels of the public service, science administration and other areas of public life. Even 20 years after most of the public turned against those policies, many of the people are still there in influential positions. They are an important part of the reason why it has been hard for New Zealand to change direction.

While pro-free-market people were being promoted, people with different views were left behind and sometimes were actively pushed out of positions of influence. The dominant business lobby group, the Business Roundtable, specialised in personal attacks and pressure against critics of the reforms. Many such targets were marginalised, their careers stalled or they literally lost their jobs.

Public interest politics has been weakened in many other ways. While political activities by PR people and industry lobbies became normalised and then widespread, political activity by other groups of people has been more or less subtly delegitimised. Many academics feel insecure criticising the government or their institutions. Public servants, scientists, medical professionals and other public employees feel insecure, if not prohibited, from taking part in politics in their spare time. Public interest groups also feel constrained from criticism and advocacy, in case it imperils public funding. Even many ordinary people wonder if it is safe to take part in protest. The result is a huge loss of people, ideas and skills from democratic politics.

The cumulative effect has been a decline and muting of voices promoting the public interest, while corporate political activism has grown exponentially. The resulting political environment helps explain why New Zealand has remained in a free-market time warp.

The most important step for being able to change the policies is changing the environment. The most practical way to do this is to strengthen the democratic and public interest infrastructure of the country. The first steps are clear and ready to be implemented.

1. Actively encourage academics, scientists and others on public salaries to participate in pressing social and political issues rather than primarily rewarding publication in academic journals.
2. Reassure all public employees of their right to be active citizens in their own time and encourage them to do so.

3. Radically restructure the public sector into a genuine, independent public service.
4. Establish publicly funded research and policy institutes oriented to the public interest.
5. Rewrite election and political party laws to minimise the influence of money in politics, including prohibiting large political donations.
6. Acknowledge the crisis in private news media and dramatically increase long-term funding and statutory independence for non-commercial television, radio and, eventually, print public news media.

The sensible starting point for democratic renewal is public institutions and public funding. Many other things can follow.

The Enduring Legacy

E. W. Thomas[1]

Introduction

This country, as with many other countries, has undergone a traumatic neoliberal transformation. A theory that insists human wellbeing can best be advanced by liberating individual entrepreneurial freedoms and skills within a framework of strong property rights, free markets and free trade has been pursued in New Zealand to a radical extent. The outcome, as in other countries that have pursued the neoliberal creed, has been extreme and even obscene inequality.

Any number of academic writers have pointed out that the process of neoliberalisation has wrought observable dislocation and hardship to many people. Take just two authors. Respected historian the late Tony Judt in his book *Ill Fares the Land*, points to the material self-interest that dominates Western societies and regrets the fact that we have lost the sense of collective purpose which was inherent in the values of social democracy.[2] In *False Dawn: The delusions of global capitalism*, John Gray focuses on the false premises that underlie neoliberalism.[3] His message is that the pursuit of United States-style capitalism – the Washington consensus and corporate driven globalisation – has led to social and cultural decay.[4]

Authors such as Judt and Gray, who deplore the spread of neoliberalism, make out a compelling argument. Yet, notwithstanding the collapse of a feral financial market on Wall Street in 2008, many people continue to endorse neo-classical economics. But such economics have proved misguided or, indeed, at times, plain foolish.

I do not intend in this chapter to recount the extreme disparity in income and wealth that now characterises Western democracies, including New Zealand. Inevitably reinforced by statistics and graphs, this disparity has been demonstrated in any number of tracts. The book edited by Max Rashbrooke, *Inequality: A New Zealand crisis*, demonstrates the explosion in the rich–poor divide during the last 30 years.[5] It can no longer be plausibly denied that the lavish lifestyle of the uber rich is obscene and that the poor are increasingly marginalised and disadvantaged. Surely it is a truism to assert that, where social and economic disparity is of this order, social justice is in serious default.

Critics of this injustice are met with the charge that inequality is inevitable and, indeed, desirable. The charge is superficial. Critics are addressing extreme or gross inequality. They accept, as do I, that a degree of inequality is inevitable and that it provides a stimulus to economic progress. Thus, the inequality under attack is the extreme or gross inequality which is the product of the neoliberal economic regime beginning in the mid-1980s.

Why is this gross inequality tolerated?

How has this extreme inequality been tolerated in a country that once prided itself on its egalitarian culture and sense of social justice?[6] The answer is simple, although unpalatable to many. This gross inequality has been fostered and sustained by the mantras, the myths, and the specious beliefs that are propagated by the rich and powerful to perpetuate their wealth and privilege. This is not to say that they do not believe the mantras and myths they propagate. For the most part, they do. Indeed, it is the fervency of their convictions that makes them such potent protagonists and determined protectors of the privileged position they have wrested from the community.

The mantras and myths

I touch upon the mantras that are used by the Right to buttress opposition to government intervention below. But there are a plethora of other myths that serve to maintain the political and economic power of the wealthier sector of society. For the most part they have been discredited by experience, disproved by statistics and studies, or debunked by most economists. 'Trickle-down' economics is a prime example. The myth that a progressive tax of the wealthy depresses production and retards economic growth is another. The notions that the poor have only themselves to blame and that a person's wealth is due *solely* to his or her own hard work are far too prevalent. Yet another myth is the perception that the country's finances are the household or family's finances writ large. And the claim that high CEO and senior executive salaries and large bonuses, even if they appear obscenely high, are essential to the operation of the free market continues to be peddled by the Right.

The basic problem is that these mantras and myths propagated by the rich and powerful to maintain the social, economic and political order are widely accepted by those who are not rich and powerful. Karl Marx described this phenomenon as "false consciousness". The insight captures the notion that people are unable to see things, whether exploitation, oppression, economic factors or social relations, as they really are. They are seduced into believing that the interests of the rich and powerful are their interests or serve their interests. Social activity and institutions making up the super-structure of society are subtly conscripted to further the interests of those privileged with wealth and power.

Theoretically, those citizens who are vulnerable to the slings and arrows of the economic order should be able to look to the political process for protection. Being representative, the government can be held accountable. But while the shortcomings of representative government should not be overstated, the reality is less attractive than the theory. The notion that vulnerable individuals and disadvantaged groups in society can obtain effective recognition in the political process is problematic. Certain sectors and special interests exercise a disproportionate influence. Money counts. So, too, does the collateral control of, or dominance in, the media count. The widespread endorsement of these mantras and myths is the result.

Historically, the welfare of the vulnerable and disadvantaged has been to some extent protected by what might be loosely described as the middle class, people at the centre of the socioeconomic spectrum. The middle class has been relatively well off and aspired to be even better off. As the perceived power-brokers in a democracy, they have been courted by the major political parties and thereby provided a moderating buttress against the exploitative potential of capitalism. I am not saying that the middle class will not continue to exert an ameliorating influence on the more extreme political agendas forever afoot in a democracy, but the middle class is also being left behind. In the United States this phenomenon is described as the 'hollowing out' of the middle class who, nevertheless, continue to reflect the values of the wealthiest 20%. Seduced by the mantras and myths purveyed by the rich and powerful, they perceive the interests of that elite to be their interests.

Yet, society is an integrated and interdependent economic and social estate, and the vulnerable and disadvantaged cannot be excluded from that estate. The woe-be-gones, the misfits and the inevitable 'losers' in a capitalistic society cannot be simply discarded on some scrap heap reserved for 'social misfits'. As human beings and members of society they are vested with rights which guarantee them the basic means of sustaining life and obtaining a reasonable quality of life.

A speech made on behalf of this country on the adoption of the Universal Declaration of Human Rights in Paris in 1948 spelt out the basic entitlements:

"[T]he right to work, the right to a standard of living adequate for health and well-being, and the right to security in the event of unemployment, sickness, widowhood and old age". Recognising that the common man and woman are social beings, the same speech emphasised that people have "the right to education, the right to rest and leisure, and the right to freedom to freely participate in the cultural life of the community". These social and economic rights can give the individual the normal conditions of life which make for 'larger freedom'. Only when there is a full recognition of economic, social and cultural rights will this larger freedom be achieved: freedom for the individual to develop in a society alert to the basic rights of the individual.

It is this larger freedom which has been derailed by neoliberalism and the commitment of that creed to neo-classical economics. As a first step, therefore, to achieving a more equal and just society, the damaging features of neoliberalism which remain must be identified and then challenged.

Neoliberalism lingers on

What, then, are the negative or subversive features of the neoliberal legacy which must be arrested and reversed? I will touch upon seven.

1. Values directed by the economic order

The first damaging feature of neoliberalism is the fact that the economic order has been permitted to direct, if not dictate, the values and morality of the community. But the morality of capitalism is a pagan morality; a morality bounded by the profit motive and the obsession with consumerism and the materialistic values it engenders. The prime example of this perverted morality exists in the fact that a person's worth is measured, not by the value of his or her contribution to the wellbeing of the community, but by their accumulation of personal wealth.

The immediate point, therefore, is simple: naked self-interest (for which it is easy to read greed) is a malign foundation for a healthy society. The free market should not be permitted to dictate or direct the values of the community. Rather, the community must determine its own values, and impose those values on the free market.

2. Exploitation

The second feature is that we have become increasingly tolerant or even immune to the most reprehensible of all social and economic evils – exploitation. The potential for exploitation is inherent in capitalism. Those with superior power, either through natural advantages, acquired knowledge, inherited wealth, or fortuitous circumstances, are in a position to take advantage of others who are vulnerable to the exercise of that power. The profit motive then ensures that someone or some sector, generally working people, will be exploited, or will be vulnerable to exploitation, to maximise the profit.

The exploitation of natural resources and the environment is again the inevitable consequence of rampant capitalism. Economic theory is based on the gospel of scarce resources. In essence, economics is all about the allocation of scarce resources. But the unregulated free market has no inbuilt mechanism that permits it to recognise that truism and so modify the avaricious profit motive that drives the system. The environment is desecrated and our natural resources depleted. Those who trumpet the mantra that the free market is the most efficient means of allocating scarce resources tend to disregard the impact of an unregulated market on the environment.[7] Yet, the true burden of the environmental cost is not borne by those who profit from the usurpation of the planet's limited resources but by the community as a whole.

3. *Equality*

The third feature relates to the concept of equality. Equality today is more often than not defined in terms of 'equality of opportunity'. Equality of opportunity has become a political mantra. It has the effect of obscuring the true extent of inequality within the community. Yet, equality must mean more than equality of opportunity. Certainly, everyone should have the opportunity to develop their talents to the full. But if equality means no more than that, it is simply the opportunity for those with a fortuitously superior genetic structure or fortuitously privileged background to advance their superiority and privilege. As a practical matter, the premise underlying equality of opportunity should be the existence of a level playing field, but gross inequality as well as genetics, ethnic and other prejudices, the economic order, and liberal individualism effectively preclude that premise.

This degraded perspective of equality in turn impairs social mobility. The disadvantaged are stuck with being disadvantaged. Upward mobility has steadily declined in the past two and a half decades. It becomes a vicious circle. Children of poorer parents are less well-educated and well-placed and obtain fewer opportunities to compete with those who are better educated and better placed. Children without an inheritance are at a disadvantage relative to those who are favoured by inherited wealth. Children of parents in a poorer area will not enjoy the advantages of their more affluent neighbours. And the children of their children will necessarily fare worse again. An unabashed evil of inequality is that it perpetuates itself and secures its own expansion.

4. Government intervention

The fourth feature relates to state intervention. The populace has been conditioned by mantras and catch-phrases to repel government intervention, whether beneficial or otherwise. The political manifestations of the unregulated free market have widespread and unquestioned support. Take a sample: blind adherence to the private sector and an equal measure of disdain for the public sector (meaning in reality a blind bias in favour of private enterprise, a blind disregard of the mixed record of private businesses, and an equally blind rejection of the contribution and worth of the public sector); 'small government' (meaning in reality fewer government policies favouring the vulnerable and disadvantaged and less government assistance for the unfortunate); privatisation is necessary for efficiency (meaning in reality a transfer of wealth from the many to the more affluent few); 'flexible labour' (meaning in reality less pay and tougher conditions for workers); 'choice' (meaning in reality choice for the better off); 'market discipline' (meaning in reality, more often than not, a savage reduction in the number of employees or the attribution of an artificial money value to an inherently unquantifiable quality of service); and the holy grail of endless growth (meaning in reality an ill-informed optimism that growth is an eternal principle).

Catch-phrases also take on the bogus status of mantras: 'the politics of envy'[8] (a phrase used to deter criticism of inequality and foster acquiescence in the status quo); 'nanny state' (a phrase used to generate a blanket resentment of all or any government intervention); and 'welfare cheats' (a label utilised to denigrate beneficiaries generally even though the great majority of beneficiaries are not cheats and are in genuine need of assistance).

It is, in short, the hyperbole of right-leaning ideologues that has convinced people it is not a good thing to interfere in the market.

In New Zealand, the leaky homes debacle provides a ready example of this misplaced ideological approach. The Bolger Government scrapped the existing controls in the building industry and instituted a 'light-handed' regulatory regime. The regime failed, and leaky homes have been the outcome at a cost to the community of $11-plus billion – and still rising.[9] Legal liability, where liability has been established, has generally been imposed on local councils. The deficit can only be made up from rates paid by the many. But the true responsibility for this expensive fiasco was the government of the day's policy to adopt a light-handed regulatory regime. The hard fact is that the strength of the profit motive and the impact of competition in the market place was discounted or ignored.[10]

It is, is it not, an incongruent mystery as to why those of a neoliberal or purest free-market disposition can at one and the same time extol the profit motive and yet fail to understand the compulsive force of that motive.

It must, therefore, be more widely appreciated that effective regulation is essential to curb the shortcomings of the free market and attain the goal of social justice. As consumers, people have a voice in the operation of the free market; as voters they can have an overriding voice in controlling the harmful effects of the free market. Regulation, in other words, is the means by which they can give effect to that voice and harness the free market to their service.

It may well be that, for the free market to operate in the public's favour, the solution in any given situation may be more competition and not more state direction or control, but the point is that government intervention is still required to bring that solution about. What is required in each case is a pragmatic determination as to which solution best serves the common good.

5. *Unemployment*

The fifth feature or concern is the fact that the community's widespread antipathy to unemployment which characterised the welfare state has diminished in intensity. Unemployment is increasingly seen as a necessary function of economic growth, an individual misfortune to be bartered to secure greater economic efficiency, and the unavoidable consequence of controlling inflation. Yet, unemployment is a loathsome scar on the body politic and a stain on any society that claims to be a civilised society. Unemployment offends the dignity of the person. It is an affront to human dignity to be regarded as, and treated like, a commodity or unit of production.

Full employment is all too often sacrificed to obtain cheaper goods by adopting technology or replacing local labour with cheap overseas labour. It took 100 years (1802–1901) and numerous Factory Acts to rid industrial Great Britain of slave labour and child labour. But, of course, although it took time, capitalism adjusted and under global capitalism the slave labour and child labour is to be found elsewhere – in countries such as India, Bangladesh, Indonesia, and Central America. Workers in the developed economies, including New Zealand, are thrust into competition with this cheap labour. Working people, it seems, have become expendable and their dignity irrelevant.

6. *Taxation*

In the sixth place, taxation has ceased to be perceived as a civic duty. Neoliberals, individualists, libertarians, entrepreneurs, and any number of shysters claim some sort of pre-tax right to their income, some even denouncing taxation as "theft". Yet, society, even a free-market and individualistic society, cannot exist without government, and government, however large or small, requires funding. Those entrepreneurs and developers who utilise public infrastructure, public amenities and public services but do not pay their fair share of taxes are, in substance and effect, receiving a subsidy from the taxpaying members of the community.

Furthermore, tax evasion is fraudulent and tax avoidance is inequitable – and, indeed, immoral. Yet, over time both tax evasion and tax avoidance have cost the community billions and billions of dollars. (The cost of welfare fraud is miniscule in comparison with the cost of tax evasion and tax avoidance.)

7. *Trade unions*

The seventh concern is the demise of the power and influence of trade unions. Trade unions emerged in industrial Great Britain to offset the inherent power of employers, both individually and as a class, and so prevent the exploitation of workers. That rationale remains sound. Individual workers cannot match the economic and political clout of their employer or the economic and political power employers wield in the structure of the economy. The imbalance is structural unless workers are able to act collectively, and society is dysfunctional for so long as that imbalance remains. It will remain, and neoliberalism will not have been finally routed, until trade unions recapture some part of the influence they have lost, principally by the restoration of collective bargaining. Good people who contribute their labour to increase the welfare and wealth of the community cannot be forever denied their just recognition and return.

Nor can equality in the workplace be measured solely by the level of the wages or salary paid. For true equality to exist, workers must be treated fairly and in good faith by their employers and possess legal safeguards to protect their interests in a manner "worthy of human dignity".[11] Rather than being perceived as a cost, workers need to be regarded as an investment, if not a stakeholder, in the industry or enterprise to which they contribute their labour. Indeed, many studies have confirmed that such enlightened treatment also increases productivity.

There is another important aspect frequently overlooked. In the past, trade unions could make a contribution to the social cohesion and sense of community in the social democracies. Of course, trade unions in their heyday behaved in a way that was at times perceived to be contrary to the public interest. I do not deny that trade unions, like all other centres of power in society, require regulation to prevent the power they wield being abused. But the point is that the decimation of the power of trade unions has denied the labour force a sense of community and, at the same time, denied society as a whole a sense of community that is inclusive of the workforce.

Social justice

Underlying all these concerns is the seemingly dwindling commitment of the community to social justice. The central core of a society dedicated to social justice is empathy, not only individual empathy, but also the empathy of a collective and inclusive community. But the liberal individualism which has taken hold seems to preclude anything more than minimal empathy for those who suffer or who are vulnerable or disadvantaged – the so-called losers in a capitalist economy. People, good people, are fully capable of empathy, as witness the response to natural disasters such as the Christchurch earthquake, but restoring or converting this capacity for empathy to the body politic is probably the most difficult challenge facing any post-neoliberal reconstruction.

That challenge must be undertaken. It cannot brook failure. This country will not rebuild a just society unless and until the lingering legacy of neoliberalism, with all its baggage of mantras and myths, is recognised for what it is, rejected as unsound and unfair, and vanquished from our political, economic and social discourse.

1 This chapter is based on the author's Bruce Jesson Lecture given in October, 2013.
2 Allen Lane, 2010.
3 Granta Books, London, 2002. See also websites such as Closer Together, Whakatata Mai www.closertogether.org.nz.
4 Many other books advance the same theme, e.g., Ferdinand Mount, *The New Few: Or a very British oligarchy* (Simon & Schuster, 2012); and Daniel Dorling, *Injustice: Why social inequality persists* (the Policy Press, 2011).
5 Bridget Williams Books, 2013.
6 See Leslie Lipton, *The Politics of Equality: New Zealand's Adventures in Democracy* (University Chicago Press, 1948).
7 Apart, that is, from ignoring the fact that the allocation of scarce resources by the free market presupposes perfect competition when, in fact, competition is frequently imperfect.

8 E.g., John Key, the Prime Minister, has denigrated the 'politics of envy', favouring the 'politics of aspiration'. Speech to the Annual National Party Conference, 3 August 2008.

9 Leaky homes will cost $11.3 billion to fix – report, *The New Zealand Herald*, 22 December, 2009.

10 Another example is the Pike River Mine disaster. See Rebecca Macfie, *Tragedy at Pike River Mine: How and why 29 men died* (AWA Press, 2013).

11 See Article 23(1) of the Universal Declaration of Human Rights.

Beliefs

Corporate Colonising

David Cooke

> It can be quite worrying, the powerlessness of the people.
>
> MARGARET DRABBLE, RADIO NZ, 25 OCT 2013

In *Spirit of 45*, Ken Loach describes the creation of Britain's welfare state and its subsequent dismantling by Margaret Thatcher. In New Zealand, in the 1980s, the Labour Government shrank the welfare state in a whirlwind of change. A decade later in Ontario, Canada, a newly elected Tory government set out to reconstruct the province. They carefully studied the New Zealand experiment, then systematically demolished large parts of public and government institutions, under the deliberately distorting slogan of "the common-sense revolution".

Such projects follow a similar pattern. They downsize government, reducing resources for the public. They casualise the workforce and lay off public sector employees, in many cases forcing workers to apply for their own decreasing numbers of jobs. They contract out services to private institutions. They cut taxes, thereby reducing revenue for the state and starving public institutions, which then need rescue by a parallel private sector. They focus endlessly on individual responsibility, with contempt for organised collective action in the form of trade unions, though organisations of (massive) capital are apparently entirely acceptable. Crucially, they sell off public institutions to private interests.

Free-market economics insists on caustic controls of selected sectors of society. While it hates regulation of business, it's very keen to impose regulation on others. So it successfully arranges for oppressive systems of accountability and measuring, for instance in performance management in workplaces, and achievement in education, as in National Standards in New Zealand. At the same time, it has pushed hard to accept no more than *self-regulation* of industries in New Zealand, which largely calls for voluntary compliance with given industries' own codes, leading to disastrous outcomes such as the deaths at Pike River. The free-market outlook is a package deal of policies, melded together into a formidable combination with a very clear goal: *private profit through corporate control of society.*

Free-market economics is not interested in the public interest, nor in private citizens to any great extent. Its beat is privately owned entities, especially corporations. It does, however, have an interest in profiting from public institutions, because they are ready-made going concerns, constructed with public resources over decades. Corporations profit both by piggy-backing on the public sector and by taking over essential areas of public life, for instance aspects of health, education and welfare, through various forms of privatising to ensure demand and profits.

These private institutions exist to make profit, for themselves and for shareholders. They are not set up to provide revenue for other institutions in society, and indeed they devote extraordinary effort to avoid funding others, known as tax avoidance. At best, they offer a form of 'trickle-down' benefits, which is an apt term, because the flow is minute. There could be various reasons for institutions like companies and corporations to exist, but within the free-market world, profit is vital.

The corporation is central to free-market economics. It drives the practice and expects the major benefits. This is not the domain of Joe's Corner Store. Corporations are huge institutions with massive resources and they are happy to increase their share.

But to achieve these powerful goals, it's important to have as much control as possible. This applies not just in the world of business and finance, though it certainly helps to have billions in cash, assets and resources, as say Shell or Google do. But corporations realise that they also need control through society. Therefore they build powerful patterns of influence and opinion-forming, e.g. through mass media, lobbying, public relations and market pressure. They also build strong relations with governments, making plain the sort of legislation they expect, and in some cases writing it. The priority in these moves is not humanitarian or altruistic. Corporations are in it for themselves.

Free-market speak

For several decades, we've been saturated with talk of free markets, free trade, liberalisation, freedom from constraint, freedom from government control, slogans like 'let's free business'. It's all part of a carefully constructed language designed to normalise free-market ideas that then become embedded in the functioning of the nation. This kind of language illustrates one of Milton Friedman's claims, that his economic outlook is "one that gives people what they want instead of what a particular group thinks they ought to want". Hovering over such a claim is its opposite, the idea of the 'Nanny State' as a constantly fostered kill-joy that supposedly exists to rob people of individual initiative and action.

The language of liberalising is just the beginning. Closely linked is continuing reference to choice, equality ('a level playing field'), a balanced approach, and an extensive terminology reinforcing the *market*. Within and beyond business, there is constant use of terms of competition, commodities, profit, profitability and productivity, the discipline of the market, privatising, enterprise and innovation. Significantly, these terms are regularly extended to areas beyond business itself – the international education market is 'highly competitive'; the public service is 'bloated and running low on productivity'; government 'stifles innovation'. In the world of work, we have become accustomed to constant rounds of review, reform, restructuring and, callously, redundancies. The free market, in other words, is long on workers losing their jobs.

Free-market language also proceeds strongly by way of oppositions and constraints of its own, waging relentless battle against claimed horrors like regulation of business (hence its campaign against the Resource Management Act). This public watchdog role goes well beyond mere complaint. Free-market economics unashamedly demonises its targets, as it does in the steady vilifying of beneficiaries, who are presented as undeserving and continually primed to 'rort the system'. It therefore helps to find a situation in crisis, which then needs a ready-made solution, conveniently supplied by free-market forces. New Zealand's social reforms were launched by a supposed financial crisis, and since then crises have arisen regularly (cost over-runs in ACC; poor results in literacy and numeracy). The technique is well understood in other parts of the world. When he was Minister of Education in Ontario in the 1990s, John Snobelen gained instant notoriety for realising the value of creating a crisis if one didn't exist at the time: "Yeah," he said, "we need to invent a crisis, and that's not just an act of courage; there's some skill involved."

The focus throughout is on creating a distinctive language that helps stamp free-market ideas on society. Part of the process is to replace existing terms with ones that carry market values. Hence as many people have noticed, patients in medical settings and students in education become clients, which redefines them as commercial entities. Likewise, citizens become consumers; rather than offer degrees, tertiary institutions create a product; and the Personnel sections of companies and ministries become Human Resources.

Corporatising

In New Zealand, free-market forces have successfully devoted single-minded effort to corporatising the institutions of society. In the social reforms of the 1980s, numbers of government agencies and departments were turned into *state-owned enterprises*, with strong corporate structures. Certain departments, such as Education, became ministries, again with corporate identities. But notably, as ministries, they are agents of the government of the day, through the active intervention of the given minister. In this way, the ministry lives its corporate life, but subject to forceful direction from the government – it is no longer at arms-length. It has become the norm for the new corporate structures to consist of vertical, hierarchical systems of oversight and control, with quite explicit top-down enforcement of authority, accountability and management.

Numerous other features of corporate life have been injected into the institutions that have evolved in the last three decades. CEOs are regularly employed on termed contracts that specify strict outcomes. Many of the new corporates have pared down their roles and employees to concentrate strongly on making policy. They then contract out the practical tasks of, say, research, background papers and report writing.

Put another way, there has been a determined focus on corporatising the ideology of society – to ensure that corporate values and structures become the norm. It is not necessarily the result of a move to convince the populace of the virtue of corporate guiding principles. They've simply been put in place.

At the same time, there has been a resolute push to insist on benefit for the corporate sector. We saw this in the deal that the Prime Minister negotiated with Warner Brothers over making part of *The Hobbit* movie in New Zealand. Whatever the advantage claimed for film production in the country, the fact is that the US corporate enjoyed at least $20m as a result of the deal, made sweeter for them by the PM changing labour laws overnight in restrictive ways.

An equally dramatic form of corporate benefit is asset sales. In this process, large chunks of publicly owned entities are sold to huge, often foreign, corporates, regardless of the fact that decades of public finances and collective effort have gone into building them. No matter what hair-splitting can be applied to the analysis, the fact is that governments have readily sold off the people's property, to the benefit of corporations.

Here we come to the role of government in free-market economics. One would like to think that as elected representatives of the people, the function of government is to protect the nation-state and its people. But successive New

Zealand governments have resolutely carried out free-market agendas, to the disadvantage of the people.

Ultimately, these developments are a way of corporatising *us*. As society becomes more and more corporate, so do we. As power and control pass to corporations, it becomes increasingly difficult to resist. Given the burdensome pressures on citizens as a result, it is not surprising if people tend to accept the power structure. It was with this kind of scenario in mind that David Korten published *When corporations rule the world*, in 1995.

Free-market economics is contradictory, based on faith rather than research, impressively self-seeking, theoretically inconsistent and anti-democratic. We can surely do better than this. One inspiring way to start is to consult *Time for Outrage*, by Stephane Hessel, which is a call to people to resist arbitrary power.

We make no apology for focusing a single book on a critique of free-market economics. The enthusiasts for the 'free market' promote its virtues 30 hours a day across media, public comment, economic analysis and political action, with unflagging zeal. Over a spectrum of statements and assumptions, free-market values get formidable support in a range of forms from blunt and overt to matter-of-fact, unobserved and unnoticed.

Some voices have raised questions. So do we.

Neoliberal Free-Market Beliefs

Ruth Irwin

Market places have been around for thousands of years – people traded goods and services long before neoliberal 'free trade' was invented. But this relatively new way of thinking about how we buy and sell products involves extra dimensions that need to be understood and critiqued.

On the one hand the ideas behind the neoliberal 'free' market are very detailed. On the other, their basis is astonishingly simple. It is this apparent simplicity that appeals to policy makers because the free market can be easily applied to many situations. Its moral justification lies in the belief that it is the fairest way to distribute *scarce* resources. It also claims to take lobbying out of the sphere of politics and into the 'apolitical' sphere of market interactions.

Rationality

For a start, the free market depends on rational players. Unlike real people, who make irrational, stupid, lazy, or romantic decisions all the time, the free market assumes that buyers and sellers always behave in a rational manner. It calls consumers and suppliers (on both sides of the buying and selling transaction) 'rational individual utility maximisers'. Rationality is assumed to increase the wealth or wellbeing of each individual person.

Rationality is not the same as self-interest. But in free-market ideology, both concepts are combined and inseparable. Rationality is always assumed to be individual self-interest. In contrast, it makes sense to live in a thriving community, where sometimes we forego self-interest in the best interests of the whole society and the health of the ecosystem. When we all live together in a happy and healthy community there is less likelihood of violence and crime, and better adaptability to unforeseen events. But none of these things is discussed in the theory.

The theory also relies on everyone being honest. Of course, as we all know, this is often not the case. But any marketplace needs people to be honest, so it's a fair demand. A related assumption is that the free market offers transparency of information. Rational consumers can only make the best decision if they have access to honest information. But under the guise of 'trade secrets' transparency is often unavailable.

Market assumptions are that rational consumers will 'choose' the best product through a whole range of rational decision-making processes. They will choose on the basis of price, accessible supply, quality, freshness and so on. There is no mention of marketing, fashion or sex appeal in the theory because they are not the basis of 'rational' decision-making. The idea is that when millions of people keep making rational choices about their consumer products, the price will be forced down. Rational, self-interested people will not pay more than they have to.

Invisible Hand

Over a large number of transactions, neoliberal free-market theory argues that the 'Invisible Hand' will 'balance' the market price as low as possible, without forcing all the producers to go out of business. Adam Smith argued in 1776 that (God's) Invisible Hand would add together all the rational consumer decisions, and 'balance' the market at a reasonable price. This argument is a major reason why neoliberalism attracts such devoted faith. The idea is that only (God's) Invisible Hand has the information to understand a balanced price and that the market is flexible to change but reduces costs for all consumers.

To illustrate how important it is for the theory to work (that every consumer makes rational decisions) try this thought experiment. Someone walks into a marketplace to buy tomatoes. They could base their choice on convenience, freshness, colour, organic production methods, local low carbon transport and a range of other rational criteria. But if they spin around, make themselves dizzy and point in a random direction to choose the tomatoes – then the price is set on absolute randomness rather than rational decision-making. If all decisions were made randomly, then the producers and shopkeepers could set the price however they liked: asking $20,000 for tomatoes, because price or self-interest is not affecting the customer's decision-making. Thus rational self-interest is vital for the theory of market balance to work.

The free market generalises from micro-economics (that make mathematical equations about specific markets) to macro-economics about the whole global economy. Bread is a good example. It is a very well established market. The 'price' is well known amongst the population and the commercial producers. It is set by a mutual understanding between buyers and sellers about the costs involved in production and supply, capital and labour costs, transport costs, the shopkeepers' overheads, and the minor variations in quality and freshness. The price of bread can be fairly well predicted and consumers will object if the price is set too high. This situation is called the balance of supply and demand, and it is a 'perfect' market. Over time, the supply curve has met the demand curve and the price has been established with transparency.

The perfect market occurs when there is an *abundance* of supply, and lots of competition between suppliers. We can see that the Invisible Hand gets to work balancing the market, and the result is the fairest distribution of bread for the lowest price, to the multitude of consumers. The moral claims are that the Invisible Hand facilitates the fairest distribution and the fairest price to consumers and producers.

The 'bottom' price is set by the irreducible costs that producers have to cover. These include buildings, electricity, water supply, machinery, production lines, maintenance, raw materials, labour costs, insurance and so on. If the price goes under the cost of production, then all the producers will go bankrupt. So in a perfect market the price hovers just above production costs, and in fact the profit really only covers the long-term costs of maintaining machinery and other capital costs.

Adam Smith and other free-market theorists have taken the specifics of very common market goods like bread, or nails, and generalised them to all global relations. As we will see, there is no justification for making such exaggerated claims from the examples of very common goods that do have perfect market situations. Common goods are not in scarce supply, and so the justification that the market is the fairest form of distribution of scarce resources is false.

The perfect market only takes place when there is an abundance of supply and an abundance of competition between suppliers and amongst consumers. When there is little supply then prices can be set by the supplier and the customer has no choice but to pay the premium. This leads to lots of profit for suppliers and an unfair situation for consumers because the Invisible Hand is unable to balance the 'perfect' market. Many market items are in this category.

Winners and losers: competition and innovation

In general, bankruptcy is not seen as a bad thing in neoliberal market theory but it is a harsh philosophy that blames the victim. Bankruptcy is the failure of a company to adapt to changing market conditions. As the perfect market takes hold, profit decreases to the point where it only maintains essential production costs. These circumstances always give rise to a lot of competition and those companies who are unable to compete go bankrupt.

Neoliberal free-market theory regards profit as proof that a company can 'win' the competition between producers. This they do by innovation which may take a variety of forms. New products command market uniqueness and that means no competition – so the producer can set a high price and make a good profit. Other forms of innovation focus on efficiency. New products, new supplies, better production methods, lower capital costs, lower wages, cheaper new materials are the most common ways of innovating to reduce costs against the competition, and increase profit. It's a very seductive story to believe that 'successful' business equals technological innovation and economic growth.

The story of winners and losers in market competition makes no mention of anti-competitive purchasing of new patents. It takes no account of the expense, risk and long timeframes of research and development – which is often a burden held by the state and universities rather than companies. Nor does the story of winners and losers discuss the difficulties for some smaller businesses to access finance for the expense of retooling. Even less discussion goes into the merits of production for a nation state's wellbeing or the damage that is caused by incredibly poor wages, conditions, and environmental impacts in offshore labour. These difficulties are simply subsumed under 'competition'.

State interference

Free-market theory takes for granted the peaceful conditions and infrastructure provided by nation states. At the same time, free-market ideology holds a generalised antagonism towards the taxes and 'interventions' that disrupt the Invisible Hand of the market.

Tax is seen as almost entirely unnecessary and unreasonably increasing costs and siphoning off profit. Tax is seen as fair game for innovation in tax evasion and as just another cost that can be handled more efficiently. Tariffs are considered even worse than tax. They are anti-competitive, giving domestic companies an unfair advantage over global competitors and disrupting the 'balance' of the Invisible Hand. In other words, tariffs which protect domestic producers (by taxing imports, for example) increase the cost of goods coming into the country and then domestic producers do not have to be as innovative or competitive with foreign producers – so the cost to consumers goes up.

State intervention is treated with such disdain that all state enterprises are considered better as private companies, where the Invisible Hand can set to work. According to free-market theory, most elements of the state can be privatised. That includes schools and other educational institutions, research, hospitals and healthcare, ACC insurance, roads, rail, public transport, water, power, protection such as police, lawyers, the army, and prisons. The few institutions and roles that neoliberalism does not have its eye on are judges and courts of law, but even these are in the process of being harshly reduced in scope. All of these state enterprises are seen as potential profit-making companies that would be 'more efficient' under the competitive regime of the Invisible Hand.

The theory's global outlook contains no sense of nationality or protection of the nation state. For example, the vast difference in living costs for labourers are irrelevant to free-market theory. Indeed, if anything, these types of differences between countries are seen as an advantage as companies can outsource their labour costs to countries with less protection for their workers and fewer laws to protect environmental damage and pollution.

Likewise, there is no consideration given to 'externalities' such as the pollution from mass transportation. Anything that is not a direct cost borne by the companies that produce the product is irrelevant to the free-market discourse. That is why climate change has been a direct outcome of free-market practices.

The only moral justification for neoliberal theory makes the claim that it is the fairest method of redistributing scarcity. However, as we all know, the rich are better able to access scarce and highly valuable market products and the poor do without. The justification for increasing disparities between rich and poor has been the 'trickle-down' effect: the rich will buy more as money flows easily for them, and this will stimulate the overall economy, making more jobs available. However, the general emphasis on efficiency leans in the opposite direction – making it important to hire as few staff as possible, to keep wages and conditions as low as possible, and to develop more efficient production and materials for products. In other words, the 'trickle down' effect was a vital element of the theory that has fallen out of use as there is no evidence it worked.

Furthermore the entire reliance on 'competition' has proven false. As companies become increasingly successful they tend to attract more and more of market share. This is not always to do with efficiency but often with familiarity, popularity and fashion – none of which are 'rational'. Larger companies are better able to retool, to cover the costs of spreading into new regions and consumers, and so on. So rather than encouraging competition on a 'level playing field', the free market actually tends towards fewer and fewer companies that are larger and more international in outreach. The theory is based on micro-economics and competition between small scale companies with basically equal access to resources. However, the reality is that larger and larger corporations make it impossible for small family businesses to compete. This is called 'monopoly' and it goes against every element of 'free competition' that is the basis of the Invisible Hand balancing the market.

Neoliberalism has no theory of finance or banking interest rates. It assumes that one dollar out is the same as one dollar in. There is no recognition of interest payments. Paying interest on loans forces companies to expand or 'grow' to cover the increasing amounts of their debt. Effectively, interest forces economic 'growth' to repay loans. Often efficiency and innovation cannot cover the shortfall between the original loan and the interest, and so 'externalities' that are unaccountable absorb the required growth. Resource depletion, unethical pollution, ruthless labour practices, and union busting all contribute to the shortfall in innovation and efficiency, as companies struggle to fulfil their financial debt obligations.

Neoliberalism is very simple. It is based on the belief that selfish rational individuals make hundreds and hundreds of consumer decisions that (God's) Invisible Hand balances into a market price. This is supposed to make the fairest redistribution of scarce resources, but in fact it only works on commonly found goods.

Companies are supposed to compete on a level playing field to create innovation and efficiency. This is supposed to bring down the price of goods and services through the Invisible Hand. However, multinational corporations have a distinct advantage over small family businesses, and markets tend towards monopoly rather than lots of competition.

Bankruptcy is seen as the fault of lousy companies that cannot compete. However, the reality is that competition fails to work and the free market favours massive corporations with no competition.

Nation states are seen as interfering and disrupting the Invisible Hand through taxes and tariffs. Although all the evidence points in the opposite direction, privatisation is considered to make state-owned enterprises more efficient and innovative.

Bank interest rates do not figure in free-market theory. In fact, interest repayment forces companies to keep 'growing' to keep pace with the interest on their debt. In the end they are reduced to ruthless measures on the environment and their workers in order to meet their loans.

The Perils of 'Public Choice'

Nesta Devine

A curious, but very influential set of ideas, is public choice theory. Put simply, it is the view that the insights of 'economics' can apply to all other forms of public life. Theory often seems remote and hard to grasp, but in this case it can be seen to have a continuing impact on our everyday lives.

Looking hard at the theory highlights its tensions and inconsistencies, because it is applied to fields where it does not naturally fit.

The major tensions are:

- The '**rationality**' of public choice theory;
- the **nature of the person** or 'individual';
- its **model of human interaction**; and
- its **model of government**

Public choice theory has its roots in the 17th-century desire for freedom from the oppression of arbitrary and sometimes vicious rulers. In the 1600s, a small but growing business class wanted to live without the restraints of taxation, tithing, customs or import duties. In that sense, the theory is the economic equivalent of the desire for a range of political freedoms: a free ballot for voting; freedom of association; freedom of the press; freedom from the billeting of soldiers. 'Public choice' thinking focuses on the economic aspect of these desires. But, ironically, it often loses sight of the political freedoms which become threatened by the emphasis on financial freedom.

Rationality/reason

Public choice theory is based on the view that 'economics' is 'scientific', and therefore 'proved' to be true, and rational. But this is a particular form of economics and of science. The test for scientific value becomes somewhat obscure – and in this case does not include evidence, which is the way Carl Menger and Milton Friedman actually see it. They explicitly reject the idea that there's any need to test or 'disprove' economics. To them, the logic of theory is enough to make it valid, and it doesn't matter if there are bad outcomes from applying the theory. Menger was one of the originators of public choice and Friedman was a strong supporter.

At heart, public choice theory is even less rational than pure theory would demand. It lies in the *Invisible Hand* made famous by Adam Smith. He claimed that the market moves "as if by an invisible hand," to convert personal wishes into success in the market place and then into national wealth. This invisible hand was visible in both words and pictures. In the church that Smith worshipped at, for instance, it is the Hand of God or Christ. In mediaeval times, it was claimed that the Hand guided the King or Emperor in their decisions, thus ensuring that both the secular power and God himself were establishing the laws for the population to observe. This religious claim for relying on markets is seldom publicly discussed.

The person – looking after number one

The original 'person' of neo-classical economics is *homo economicus*, who is by nature eternally self-seeking, with a constant desire for *more*. In this form of economics, the self-seeker is the only form of being. All other ways are dismissed as somehow primitive or mad – "not a man to us," as Friedrich Hayek put it. Therefore other lives don't count: female, non-greedy, collective, tribal, for example. This person, *homo economicus*, is then imposed on everyone's lives at all levels: the business person, the employee, the public servant, the unemployed person.

But in this theory, the worker, the civil servant and the out-of-work all face strong disapproval. The employee is likely to rip off the business owner. The public servant *by definition* exploits the taxpayer (by requiring higher pay, a bigger office, more employees). And the unemployed or ill person is just a 'beneficiary', i.e. a drain on the taxpayer.

Everyone, then, is reduced to economics, and therefore loses connections to land or tribe or ideas or vocation. All these aspects of a person's 'preferences' can be reduced to finances. Where then, would unselfish, active concern for others' welfare fit into this scenario? How does one account for altruism – for a person acting in the interests of others rather than in their own best interests? There are two possible responses. One is to regard altruism as simply troublemaking, interfering with the efficient process of the market. The other is to regulate altruism as an aspect of government social welfare.

Currently, governments like the idea of replacing social welfare with charity, which is one form of altruism. One way of doing so is through tightly controlled gifting from the rich and from charitable organisations. In New

Zealand, the public-sector reformer Rod Deane recommended managing the government's social welfare along the lines of the New Zealand Society for Intellectually Handicapped Children. The IHC used voluntary workers instead of paid ones, and was therefore considered far more 'efficient' than other forms of welfare provision. The increasing 'professionalisation' and control of charities through the Charities Commission is part of this push to use altruism to replace social welfare.

To market, to market: the model of human interaction

Hayek thinks human institutions are involved in a struggle to find the 'fittest' – a form of 'social Darwinism'. In his view, the survivors throughout the years are the market, the church and the family. Oddly, he then neglects the church and family completely, and recommends remodelling all other institutions on the basis of the market. There are apparently a number of advantages: the market (through the 'invisible hand') acts as a kind of evolutionary sorting house. Only the 'fittest' products, manufacturers and financiers will survive the sorting procedure. That is the 'discipline' of the market.

Moreover all participants are equal – one person's dollar is only as good as the next person's dollar, so both are equal in the market. This is true democracy. Some people will have more dollars than others, but that is seen as a good thing. Why? Because it gives people the incentive to take part in the market, either by selling products or their own labour. That way they increase their own wealth and that of the nation.

As a result, there is no economic reason to be concerned about poverty. And government shouldn't intervene, because that would interfere with the market's ability to bring about improvement. These ideas, especially worship of the market, support the principle of 'user pays'. Part of the reasoning here is that it is immoral to require the taxpayer to pay for a service they do not take advantage of. Moreover, it is also inefficient, because private business cannot compete with the power and resources of government.

Government: the 'problem' of democracy

Public choice theory is not enthusiastic about democracy or democratic procedures. By and large it is out to protect the freedom of 'taxpayers' to spend their own money. That leaves those who are not 'taxpayers' or wealthy out in the cold. The underlying idea is that democracy is seen as a way in which the poor (of whom there are many) will spend the resources of the wealthy (of whom there are few). The implication is that the poor will spend recklessly because they haven't 'earned' this money.

The essence of 'public choice' is that the public (which means taxpayers/the wealthy) have the choice over where and how to spend their money.

So public choice theory clearly sees democracy as a problem and proposes several ways of dealing with the issue.

'Constitutional economics' has several prongs. The first is to replace the rule of parliaments or elected bodies like congress with 'the rule of law'. In this scenario, a primary principle would reduce all debate to a specific question, which would be previously mandated – a rule like 'All decisions should be fair'. Public choice adherents consider that all current political and parliamentary debate is simply a means by which various sectors of *homo economicus* pursue their own current advantage. A rule would put an end to debate, and to parliaments. Unfortunately it would also cement into place the privilege of those who were already privileged. Any objection would be seen as an objection to 'fairness' or 'justice'.

Constitutional economics also includes cutting decision-making down to a single person. It is very efficient. And it requires the least amount of collaboration. We could see this model clearly in the appointment of Gerry Brownlee as Czar of the Christchurch rebuild after the devastating earthquakes of 2010 and 2011 (Brownlee became Earthquake Recovery Minister). No energy or resources were to be wasted on collaboration or negotiation between interested parties. The obvious cost is that it ushers in authoritarian rule. Commentators noted that Minister Brownlee got war-time powers that can remove local government and representative democracy in one step.

Another move along these lines is to replace government funding with 'user pays'. This lightens the load for the taxpayer, and ensures that the payer is putting their dollar or vote where their advantage is. On the surface, such a move is attractive, until one analyses the effects. Take health care, for instance. Strictly, under 'user pays' we would each be responsible for paying for our own health. So those with inferior health would need to pay more than those with lucky health. And the sick would need to take out health insurance to cover themselves. But, to look at just one possibility, those with good health may have contributed to environmental damage (e.g. through creating pollution) that has helped make others sick. And those with poor health may not have enough income to buy health insurance, so they would just continue to get sick.

Considerations of inequality and fairness led countries like New Zealand and Canada to bring in single-payer health schemes during the 20th century.

These schemes recognise that collective sharing of resources and revenue provides equity and health for the bulk of their populations, and helps build nations that are socially healthy in other ways.

A third move is to decrease the size of the government. No matter how well run a government service is, it is assumed to be bloated by self-interest and vice, precisely because it is not subject to the 'discipline' of the market. There's a simple answer here. Fewer representatives means less democracy. It also means harder work for those remaining in a legislature, or fewer and less useful outcomes for the public. And the restriction of government services impacts directly on those who are most at risk in our society. Health, housing, education, and social welfare are all vulnerable to the 'public choice' desire to reduce the 'size of government'.

A further move is to replace the decision-making functions of government with referenda. The theory holds that the referendum seeks the views of all those who are going to have to pay the costs of a measure. So theoretically, it restrains governments from assuming that taxation funds are theirs to do what they like with. In the real world, there are much greater dangers. Referenda provide an excellent opportunity for loud, powerful and wealthy forces to pressure and influence the rest of society. But neither of these parties, wealthy or otherwise, has the responsibility of enacting any resulting laws. And at the same time, politicians can wash their hands of responsibility, because they can then say it's the will of the people.

The irony is that these 'solutions' end up conflicting with the very individual freedoms that public choice theory says it is promoting.

Freedom and public choice

Public choice theory uses a language of 'freedom' and 'the individual', just as traditional political liberalism does. But the terms take on different, twisted meanings. Freedom in this case refers to the freedom of the wealthy to spend their own money. This way they don't have to agree to using taxes to provide social services, which are thought to be important only to the non-wealthy. And in this kind of economics, the individual becomes a very narrow, self-interested kind of person. It's a very limited idea of the many possibilities of human nature – restricted culturally, ethically, and in gender.

Meanwhile, the functions of government are limited to two: 'defence' and 'information'. Then all other forms of national engagement can be handed over to the private sector to provide.

Public choice theory is not for the public. The choice is for the wealthy. And the 'theory' is highly dubious.

A History of Our Times

John Minto

Neoliberalism is just a strange name for a (strange) set of economic policies.

Most of us had never heard the word, until in the mid-1980s it was used to describe the radical economic policies of the newly elected 1984 Labour Government.

In that government, David Lange's Minister of Finance, Roger Douglas, led the drive to put the new policies in place without any public debate or discussion.

Most of us were confused at first because we thought Labour would bring in policies to make things easier for families. But things quickly got worse, and then they got really ugly.

There were mass redundancies and tens of thousands of people were out of work. Before, when unemployment went up, government departments would take on more workers in areas like the Railways and Ministry of Works, where there was always important work to do. But this time Labour let unemployment skyrocket and instead of taking on more workers, the government departments themselves made people redundant. Many departments were turned into SOEs (state-owned enterprises) that had to make a profit at the same time as they provided services. Most of these SOEs were then sold by the government to wealthy private investors, so those with money could make more profit.

Today we are still living under these economic policies. Both our largest political parties, Labour and National, follow them despite the dreadful harm they have done to New Zealand families and whole communities.

So where did it all start?

Back in the 1930s, the Great Depression put millions of people around the world out of work, creating widespread hunger and struggle. Capitalism had failed, but it prompted new ideas for changing the economy. One model that later developed was neoliberalism. At first it was similar to previous practices, but then it changed to mean more extreme 'free-market' policies.

The wealthy around the world wanted free-market policies, because it would mean higher profits and help the rich get richer. Two economists in particular pushed very hard for the new concept:

- Milton Friedman from Chicago
- Friedrich Hayek from Austria

Together with the backing of wealthy people, they pushed their ideas through seminars and books. Behind the scenes, they strongly influenced the wealthy, but knew it would be very hard to get their policies accepted in a democracy.

Where did it lead?

Hayek and Friedman finally got their chance in 1973 in Chile's military coup, when General Pinochet took power, with US backing, from the democratic government of Salvador Allende. With elections banned, Friedman's and Hayek's supporters got control of the Chilean economy and forced their policies onto the country.

Other advocates targeted key people in governments around the world, concentrating on converting people of influence. In Britain, they persuaded leaders in the government of Conservative Prime Minister Maggie Thatcher to use their ideas from the early 1980s, and the same with US Republican President Ronald Reagan from 1981.

It was during this time that the notorious slogan *There is no alternative* came into widespread use.

In New Zealand, people like Roger Douglas promoted free-market beliefs behind the scenes when Labour was in opposition. Then in 1984, National Party Prime Minister Rob Muldoon called a snap election before the Labour Party had formed its economic policies. Labour won, at which point, Roger Douglas used his position as Minister of Finance to force through radical policies without Labour or New Zealanders ever having discussed them.

At first people were confused and didn't understand why Labour was acting in the way it did. Douglas said it was because the previous government had borrowed too much and we needed to pay back loans quickly. He also said "there is no alternative", so opposition to these changes was weak – especially from the trade union movement, which continued supporting Labour even when the policies started hurting families really badly.

It was soon clear that senior Labour MPs such as Richard Prebble, David Caygill, Mike Moore and Michael Bassett, an all-powerful group within Labour, were all pushing these policies very hard.

For six years they wreaked havoc on the lives of low- and middle-income families. Douglas admitted later that he deliberately rushed through these policies because he knew New Zealanders would not support them, so he had to work quickly to keep critics on the back foot and make it hard to change back in the future.

The links between these Labour leaders and very wealthy individuals in New Zealand became obvious and it was clear the rich were profiting enormously. If National had tried these policies, then it's likely the whole country would have opposed them, but because the changes were led by Labour, voters felt railroaded, without anyone to turn to. This was one of the main reasons New Zealanders opted to change to MMP (Mixed Member Proportional) voting in 1994, because that would make it easier for other parties besides Labour and National to get into parliament.

In Labour's second term – 1987 to 1990 – the party began selling large government assets to wealthy investors. Such 'privatisation' made the rich fabulously wealthy. For example, Telecom was sold in 1990 for $4.25 billion to two American companies, Bell Atlantic and Ameritech. In the next 10 years, they took $12 billion in profits from New Zealanders, and then sold the company back to other private investors for another $12 billion. We were left with low-quality phone services, very expensive and slow broadband, and we are still trying to catch up with other countries today.

Where is it now?

By the time Labour was voted out in 1990, it had trashed the welfare state, introduced GST (a tax on the poor), reduced taxes on the wealthiest people, forced students to pay big fees for their education, sold our major state assets and left huge numbers of people unemployed. In the process, it made the rich super-rich at the expense of the rest of us. Labour had gone further and faster with these radical economic policies than any other country in the world. We had the fastest growing gap between rich and poor in the world from the 1980s to 2000.

From a country which was regarded so highly because of our welfare state in the 1930s, we were now an experiment in what happens when you go fast in the opposite direction.

Labour was able to keep support because it had better policies than National on anti-apartheid and anti-nuclear issues and supported gay rights. This kept many in Labour happy because they got the changes they wanted while workers and their families took the big hits.

When the 1990 election came, voters had had enough of Labour and voted National. Unfortunately National supported all the bad policies Labour had put in place. It then made things worse by smashing workers' rights to bargain for better pay and conditions (the Employment Contracts Act) and by slashing welfare benefits.

The same pattern continued for five elections – from 1984 to 2000.

Today both Labour and National still support free-market policies. National continues to sell assets and make it even harder for workers and unions to get fair employment. Labour is talking about taking more control of the economy to give workers a better deal, but one has to wonder if they have any plans to make a significant difference for New Zealand families.

Meanwhile, a really sobering outcome is 270,000 children living in poverty and a dreadful housing shortage, with people paying high rents for cockroach-infested caravans. Worst of all we have a government which is not concerned with these developments.

One way to break out of this mould is through pressure within our organisations – trade unions, churches and community groups – for policies which demand change. We all need to give active support to public campaigns to get rid of neoliberalism wherever it is in control.

To quote the late Nelson Mandela:

> Overcoming poverty is not a task of charity, it is an act of justice. Like Slavery and Apartheid, poverty is not natural. It is man-made and it can be overcome and eradicated by the actions of human beings. Sometimes it falls on a generation to be great. You can be that great generation. Let your greatness blossom.

Timeline

1984 – Labour wins with David Lange as leader.
Finance Minister Roger Douglas starts extreme free-market policies ('Rogernomics').
The dollar is 'floated'.
Currency dealers make huge profits.
Massive deregulation begins (easier for companies to make profits without rules or regulations to control them or their behaviour).

1987 –Labour wins again, continues free-market policies.
Begins selling big government companies to wealthy private investors (privatisation).
Wages stagnate.
Big industries are closing.
Unemployment skyrockets, to an all-time high of 11% in 1991
Student fees increase dramatically.
Labour introduces GST at 10% then increases it to 12.5%.

1990 – National wins.
Free-market policies continue.
More asset sales.
Employment Contracts Act hits unions and workers very hard.
Real wages fall dramatically.
National slashes income for beneficiaries.
Poverty levels rise sharply.

1993 – National wins again.
Keeps free-market policies.
The decline in voter turnout begins.
New Zealanders vote to change to MMP,
to stop National and Labour dominating the government.

1996 – The first MMP election.
Many voters turn to the Alliance and New Zealand First.
Winston Peters goes into coalition with National.
The free market thrives.

1999 – Labour under Helen Clark voted in with the Alliance.
Puts in place some small changes but keeps free-market policies.

Continued

2002 – Labour wins again under Helen Clark.

Some changes made.

'Working for Families' makes life a bit easier for working families, but not for beneficiaries.

Free-market policies maintained.

2005 – Helen Clark wins narrowly.

Keeps free-market policies.

2008 – National elected, John Key as Prime Minister.

The free market continues.

2011 – National re-elected.

Starts privatising state assets again (energy companies, Air New Zealand)

National further weakens workers' rights.

Launches more attacks on beneficiaries.

The Invisible Hand

Dylan Horrocks

COME STEP INTO THE EXCITING AND DYNAMIC WORLD OF NEO-LIBERAL ECONOMICS!
... WHERE MARKETS CONSIST OF AN INFINITE NUMBER OF SMALL TRADERS AND WELL-INFORMED CUSTOMERS, RESPONDING RATIONALLY TO SHIFTS IN SUPPLY AND DEMAND!
SMITH & SONS
BAKERS
ye Artifan Shoppe
BLACK
WHY IS EVERYONE WEARING SEVENTEENTH CENTURY COSTUME...?

...WHERE AN 'INVISIBLE HAND' ENSURES OUTCOMES THAT BEST SERVE THE GENERAL GOOD...
WAIT A MINUTE! WHERE ARE THE HUGE TRANSNATIONAL CORPORATIONS?!
WHAT ABOUT THE ROLE OF MARKETING?

er... DON'T WORRY ABOUT SUCH TRIVIAL LITTLE EXCEPTIONS! LOOK AT THIS BEAUTIFUL AGGREGATE DEMAND CURVE!!
AS
Price Level
P1
P
AD1
AD
Y
Y1
YOU'RE A FAKE! THIS IS STUPID!
IT'S NOT HOW THE REAL ECONOMY WORKS!

BUT IT COULD BE! IF WE JUST TAKE THE REFORMS FURTHER- EXPUNGE EVERY LAST TRACE OF STATE INTER-VENTION! LIBERATE THE POWER OF MARKET FORCES - WAIT! DON'T GO!
BOLLOCKS.
I'M OUT OF HERE!
WHAT A MORON!
SHEESH!

MEANWHILE...
SEE? I TOLD YOU IT WOULDN'T WORK FOR LONG! SO WHAT NOW, SMART GUY?
SIGH. OH WELL, BACK TO GOOD OLD-FASHIONED POLITICAL REPRESSION, I GUESS...
PLEASE COME BACK!
BIG BUSINESS
DYLAN HORROCKS

Outcomes

The Economy of Mana

Mānuka Hēnare

The free-market system

The underlying social and functional values of the free market are problematic for Māori kinship, ethics and values relating to work. The Employment Contracts Act (ECA) of 1991 claimed to ensure an efficient New Zealand labour market, but it merely carried out the economic reforms of the early 1980s. Little New Zealand research has been done on the cultural impact of ethics and values built into a range of related ideas: an efficient labour market; the commodification of labour; valuing capital over labour; principles of supply and demand; the motivating power of self-interest; 'utility-maximisers'; and the free market. Together, these principles, values and ethics represent a particular cultural concept and world view.

In this context, it is crucial to examine the effect of the commodification of labour on Polynesian culture, including Māori. As a result of the ECA, human labour is reduced to a mere commodity and New Zealand workers are forced to accept a fluctuating compensation irrespective of individual and collective (whānau-hapū-iwi) needs.

According to the free-market view, individuals and whānau–hapū–iwi kinship groups are motivated primarily by self-interest, and respond to the laws of supply and demand. The effect of these attitudes and behaviour on Māori is to reduce Māori and their culture to mere instruments of the economy. This, however, is not a new story for Māori, as historically, settler governments assumed and planned that Māori would be the skilled labour for the settler economy. This becomes clear in the type of schooling and tertiary education offered to Māori. Traditionally, that is not how Māori understood the nature and the purpose of an economy.

The economy of Mana – whai hua mana

The early Māori economy served both material and spiritual needs. The Māori tribal mode of production gave rise to the *Economy of Mana*, an economy of affection that considers spiritual and human ancestors and descendants not yet born. It prioritises holistic wellbeing and creating value over 'profit maximisation'. In this framework, economic action is not motivated by individual profit alone, but is embedded in a range of spiritual, ecological, social, and cultural considerations that allow for redistributing opportunities and benefits. Reciprocity was expected and was driven both structurally and spiritually. These considerations are not possible in the market economy and where the Anglo-NZ state action has dominated the process of redistribution.

The Māori economy is primarily concerned with the problems of *reproduction* rather than production. Work, or improved productivity, is not an end in itself. In contrast with the dominant work ethic in New Zealand – live in order to work – in the economy of mana it is *work in order to live*. In the traditional Māori economy, different layers of society tended to be based on control of the means of reproduction. But the free-market economy has led to stratifying society, so that the Māori 'bread basket' economy of the 1820s has shifted to become the 'basket case' it is today. As long as Māori remain rural landholders in outlook, the social structure will reflect their relations to the means of reproduction and will be evident in resulting forced inequality, poverty, and falling living standards.

In New Zealand, capitalism was developed with a history at times of significant state intervention, the welfare state being an example. In recent years, there has been a greater emphasis on the free market, and more extreme policies regarding total deregulation. Academic researchers have highlighted the psychology of Māori economic life, by which Māori have made use of the wealth they have acquired and subsidised inputs from settler governments to support whānau, hapū and iwi activities. Rather than consider these decisions as wasteful or irrational, we need to take seriously the wisdom of the investments made in maintaining positions in kinship, community, and religious networks.

Based on the social logic of the tribal mode, the economy of mana negates many of the power relationships that characterise the New Zealand economy. In the economy of mana, there is an element of reciprocity that is structurally based. Where a strong tribal mode exists, there is an economy other than the market economy. It is likely that the economy of mana has been maintained and defended against the intrusions of the market economy. Studies show that the market economy has not unilaterally destroyed the economy of mana. As seen in many economies in Africa, mana economies have the ability to survive and also affect the mode of production of the market economy.

It is only fairly recently that there has been questioning of labour legislation in relation to the Treaty of Waitangi, along with Māori views and behaviour in the economy and in work. In conventional analysis, we lack a Māori theory of economic development. For too long, it has been easy to explain away the decline in Māori prosperity as simply the gap between Māori and Anglo-Western economic frameworks – and measured only by the Western viewpoint. On the one hand, there is growing acknowledgement that Māori economic practices differ from recent dominant Anglo-New Zealand models. But on the other, there remains an assumption that conventional Anglo-Western business ideology can be applied to indigenous frameworks without modification (for example, the 'trickle down' theory). It is Māori who are expected to adapt.

A crisis of ethics

The world view of the free-market system is a mechanistic one in which human labour is valued solely for its economic purpose. The approach adopted by the market's most ardent supporters places capital and other material resources at the centre of economic activity, rather than the people in society. It contains a vision of an atomised society consisting of individuals serving and meeting their own interests.

In today's context, there seem to be two contending modes of production which influence economic structures as well as social formations. Māori history teaches us that New Zealand's Pākehā political economy has a long way to go in coming to grips with the social and cultural realities of Māori New Zealand. While Māori may have lost control over the means of production – land, capital, and know-how – a modicum of control over their labour remains. We see this control in Māori worker attitudes and behaviour that persist in the economy of exploitation. The attitudes and behaviour represent an alternative set of ethics and values that contrast and contest the frame of the ECA and the free market of the 1990s. From a Māori viewpoint, there is a crisis of ethics and values in the market place and in the labour legislation. This is unlikely to change until a more humanistic approach is adopted in managing the economy and the relationship between management and worker.

Joan Metge comments that contemporary Māori prefer to emphasise the interrelatedness of all sectors of social life, that Māori dislike compartmentalising and strictly separating one role from another. Māori commonly carry the concerns and personal relations of one sector of life into others. According to Māori, a person is one, whether at work or at play. A Māori is a Māori all the time. Metge says that this attitude is often a point of contention with Pākehā, who tend to make clean-cut distinctions, for instance between work and private life, and expect Māori to confine their Māoritanga to that private life.

The free-market system enforces individual needs and rights over those of the whānau-hapū-iwi and thereby fails to take into account the bicultural, multicultural, and ambicultural nature of New Zealand society. The utilitarian values rooted in the free-market system raise doubts about whether there can be any free public expression of intrinsic Māori values in the workplace.

Yet a labour contract relationship involves the business of gift-making and exchange. Human labour and culture are given in return for continued employment and wages incorporating the nurturing of tapu and mauri, and the enhancement of mana of all involved. The relationship involves the hau of persons and the hau of the work place. It is the respect and care of these essences and attributes of being human that lead to the growth of self-worth, dignity, pride and identity. Caring for the hau of the workplace environment maintains the tapu-mana-mauri-wairua of the context of work. This safe environment ensures productive human activity. Its values are consistent with the practices of the past.

Hau could be the contribution of Polynesian thought and practice towards healthy labour relations – management and worker need not be rivals. The theory of hau is also a theory of solidarity. Today reciprocal exchange could form the basis of both the economies of affection and the market.

The free-market system needs to be analysed in terms of the free-market frame currently so dominant. Its underlying social and functional values represent a new order that emphasises a rules-based approach to the organisation of the social order. It leaves little space for the application of Māori metaphysics and ethical responses to social, political and economic planning. Recent employment legislation mirrors the crisis of ethics and values in Aotearoa New Zealand.

What then does Māori ethics have to offer at this time? It offers a distinctive humanism. Māori philosophy proposes that human beings have a dignity (tapu and mana) and that persons are more important than capital. Therefore workers are never to be instruments, or objects, in the production process, but rather they are to be treated as the subjects of work and employment. A popular Māori proverb points to a distinctive humanistic approach:

He aha te mea pai?	What is the most important good?
Māku e ki atu	And I respond,
He tangata, he tangata	Humanity! Humanity! Humanity!
He tangata.	

Conclusion

The free market is sold to us as the institution that best allows people to focus on profit and comfort, which is the idea behind 'utility maximisers'. It is argued that this type of market is the best regulating device for transforming desire for gain into socially useful activity. The theory claims that such a market frees people from the constraints of the past, and that rather than virtue, it is enlightened self-interest that motivates people. In their quest for the best deal, the market mechanism, ruled simply by supply and demand, regulates economic activity. This is the hidden hand at work and society as a whole is said to benefit.

This view of humankind and society fails to meet not only Māori but also Polynesian criteria for economic, social and cultural advancement. I suggest that Māori philosophy and ethics offers another critique of today's economic paradigm and the labour laws that go with it. Here are some fundamental traditional Māori values and ethics – a fabric of moral sentiments – appropriate to wellbeing in economics, work and employment:

- Tapu as a theory of being
- Mana as a theory of power, authority and ends
- Mauri as a theory of life and its causation
- Hau as an integrative theory of life force and economics that involves obligatory reciprocity and social relationships
- Kotahitanga as a theory of human solidarity

Work in Danger

Helen Kelly & Peter Conway

The following interview was framed in a very poignant way. Just as we sat down to talk, Helen received a text reporting another death in the forestry sector, which the Council of Trade Unions (CTU) has campaigned vigorously to reform in the recent past.

In free-market economics, labour is a commodity – you buy in the labour you need. It's a buyer–seller market rather than a relationship market, where both parties should be getting something, equal power and mutual benefit.

This system sees employment law and employment protection as negative – interference in the free market, rather than as a social pact. It has very much restricted the rights and the protection for working people, resulting in a dramatic decline in the conditions of work and wages. The whole free-market push has become a substitute for a much more personal human relationship. It's lessened the value to both parties, employers and workers.

Employers are not getting the same annual high-wage type of skills which the economy or the leaders encourage. Instead it's low wages and deregulation. They call it "flexibility", we call it "insecurity". That's how you can win in this market: by being cheap and nasty, instead of building relationships.

Making labour a commodity has a big effect on your perspective. A surplus product can sit in a warehouse. But surplus people means unemployment. Cutting costs to make cheap products is one thing. But cutting costs for labour means contracting out and other ways to cheapen the price of labour. There's huge human consequences in allowing a free market to operate like that.

For labour, free-market economics started in the mid-80s with the Labour Relations Act, which protected some union rights, but meant that collective bargaining became a lot more restrictive. And then in the 90s, National came in essentially saying, we've dealt with supplementary minimum prices, asset sales, a floating exchange rate and changing state-sector bargaining. Now for labour law.

The 1991 Employment Contracts Act (ECA) came in at the same time as massive cuts in benefits. The National Government was determined to drive down household income one way or another. The Act basically created a contract, not a relationship. There was no obligation to bargain, nor any means for doing so. It allowed employers to offer workers individual employment agreements.

In industrial relations, we used to talk of three stools. One was 'compulsory unionism'. That meant that half of the workforce joined unions. The second was 'blanket coverage through an award', meaning a registered union was entitled to bargain with employers. That was then enforced by statute with all other employers in the same occupation or industry. And the third was 'arbitration', meaning if you couldn't resolve something, you'd go to a third party and the court would decide.

Arbitration went in the 80s, the others in 1991. The award system had provided a statutory minimum for thousands of workers, so it was very damaging when it went. That's because there was a supermarket award in the supermarket sector, food awards in food retailing, then butchers, metal trades, store workers, drivers. They set out minimum rates of pay and conditions that applied by law to every employer and employee in business in each sector. This gave the award system tremendous strength and coverage.

So there was still the minimum wage as a bottom floor in the labour market, and these industry documents above it, as a second floor. But the National Government took away the second floor, froze the minimum wage, and promoted individual contracts. The idea was to move away from collective bargaining in industry. The only positive things in the ECA were personal grievance provisions to appeal against unfair dismissal, and the requirement to ratify the results of collective bargaining. That's two good things and about 200 bad things in the Employment Contracts Act. It was a radical dismantling of our wages system, which is what it's actually about – the wages system.

Take it or leave it

In the case of *Tucker Wool Processors Ltd v Harrison & Ors* [1999], workers at a wool processing plant that was being sold wanted their union to negotiate their terms and conditions with the new employer. Instead, the employer offered individual contracts on a "take it or leave it" basis. To keep their jobs the workers had to agree to an inferior contract, losing many of their old conditions and with many unreasonable new conditions.

The Court of Appeal[1] said that this was what the ECA was intended to do: "The policy and wording of the 1991 Act make it clear that either party to the negotiation may, in general, proceed on a 'take it or leave it' basis".

1 *Tucker Wool Processors Ltd v Harrison & Ors*. Unreported CA 260/98 at p. 23.

Then they deregulated. Take forestry. Previously, the workers were all under a single employer, they had a union and collective agreements. Then forestry was sold to Carter Holt Harvey and Fletchers, who broke them into multiple units, which are now owned by foreign investors. These big companies dispersed the workforce into 300 contracting companies. The workers now have no bargaining rights, no ability to organise and often aren't even provided proper health and safety gear, like wet-weather gear, or work-breaks or shelter. There's no maximum hours of work for any worker in New Zealand. They can just work and work and work, while wages get lower and lower and lower. People are working longer and longer hours. It's taking people's lives.

You have to remember that it's about capitalism getting its greatest return from work – it doesn't want anything to get in the way. But collectivised labour puts a brake on that.

Effects of free-market economics

Some of the effects of the free market in New Zealand are 300,000 people earning on or near the minimum wage, with no bargaining mechanism. The minimum wage is not a liveable wage. Then there's the health and safety record – six times as bad as the UK and twice as bad as Australia. And there's the wage gap with Australia – about 20–30% drop over the last 15–20 years.

Commodifying hits both work-life balance and beyond. Working conditions are inhumane, considering the kind of labour demanded, the lack of safety controls, the hours of work. The reward has been very minimal, and on top of that you're trying to juggle commitments to children, to family and to community. That's becoming increasingly difficult in a 24/7 world, where there are no boundaries. There's great insecurity. Is there enough income? Will you have a job? How many hours will it be? Will it be permanent or external or very casual? People's time gets chopped up into little bits that are of value to an employer, but which destroy the quality of life for workers.

Just as bad, all the risks shift to the worker: the risk of redundancy, lack of training, lack of skill investment, financial, health and safety. One new form of hiring is *triangular employment* – companies, contractors and labour. The construction companies benefit from all the labour, they get their buildings built, but they virtually employ nobody. They contract it all out to contractors and subcontractors. The employer avoids any of the responsibilities of employment, such as health and safety, the right to wage setting, a union on site. Workers are just rented out by the day like machines.

Lots of contracts set workers' rosters each week, but with no guaranteed hours. We don't call them 'zero contracts', but that's effectively what they are. Typically they can require some one to be available for up to 60 hours a week, with hours to be confirmed each week. There's absolutely no regulation of hours of work.

This deregulation of the labour market has two outcomes. One is that many workers have become dependent on legislation for the minimum wage, holidays or health and safety rather than collective bargaining. The other is that the burden of low wages has fallen back on the tax system. Government has had to step in with *Working for Families*. That's going to reach a saturation point, because it's an unsophisticated way of setting wages and conditions. But also the taxpayer cannot continue to supplement low wages, because people then don't pay taxes. It's a vicious circle.

Yet these are hugely profitable companies paying some of the lowest wages – supermarkets, forestry, farming (the most productive sector in New Zealand). In Australia, the most productive, highly valuable sector – e.g. mining and construction – pays good wages. In New Zealand it's the opposite. When everybody is reliant on the minimum code and there are no maximum hours of work, workers make up the shortfall for low income by having two jobs and working long hours.

In free-market talk, the language about labour tells you a lot. An employer is somehow a charitable organisation gifting jobs. That makes workers beneficiaries of the job, meaning they would be ungrateful to organise and seek better conditions. Another image or 'narrative' is *willing seller–willing buyer*. We've had that from the Prime Minister, arguing against the right of disabled people's caregivers to get the minimum wage.

A third story is that unions are an interloper, rather than an organisation of working people themselves. Ironically, in forestry of all things, there's a lot of effort put into painting unions as the exploiters of the workers. This industry, which is killing dozens of workers, says that somehow unions exploit them by wanting better terms and conditions. The narrative about unions is always that they're 'self-interested', out for their own power. Part of that is a move to picture unions as different from workers. So workers get together, they form a union, they pay an official to do some work for them – and then that's played as the official taking control of the workers.

It's the language of 'union bosses'. We're tolerated if we're weak. If we're ever strong, then it's a major problem: you cannot have strong unions. What will they do with that strength? We'll get unreasonably high wages and we'll disrupt things. It's all part of the narrative about unions that's quite shocking in this country, when actually we are non-profit organisations of working people who stand for a set of values that include the power of the collective group.

Take it or leave it

- A timber worker fell asleep while driving home after several consecutive 17-hour shifts. After his death, the Coroner criticised the employer for structuring shifts in such a way under the man's employment contract.
- During a meeting between the union and senior management of a large company to discuss union claims, staff in 82 branches were simultaneously being shown a video outlining their new contract. This had been written solely by the employer who invited staff into the office one by one to sign it.
- A worker with 23 years' service in an industrial cleaning company lost all service-related entitlements, and had to sign an inferior contract when the business was sold to a new employer.
- The managers of one government department called staff and offered them a one-off payment on the basis of leaving the union and signing an individual contract.
- One home-care employer insisted on a new contract for every new client a worker wanted to take on. To get the client, the care-worker needed to sign the contract.

We've got a so-called right to strike, but it gets chipped away daily. The employer's view is that you shouldn't ever use it. But employers can exercise their rights – of dismissing workers, laying off thousands – when it's more profitable to do so. There's no sense of equivalence, of human rights for workers to organise collectively. And there's no recognition that working people have an economic interest in the quality of their work. The idea is that someone else picks up the social costs – either the state or families or communities.

Just imagine a different vision that sees workers acting collectively to advance the interests of communities. The communities would be healthier, jobs would be better, and wages would be higher. There'd be a better share of profits across the community and a whole lot of social effects from that, like more stable households and kids going to school more regularly. Communities would be connecting with each other because there'd be time for them to connect.

Regulation

Look at regulation – first, with a small 'r'. We would promote things like government procurement with industries that are good employers, who make New Zealand products and create New Zealand jobs. There'd be guidelines when the government buys, to make it take into account New

Zealand content, plus sustainability and innovation.

Then there's big 'R' Regulation, which sets out what the state expects of any party in society, including unions, employers, workers, training institutions. One of the big failures in a deregulated economy is that there's very little industry training going on. Take cooking. We've got 80 workers engaged in a full cooking qualification in this country. Yet we've got hundreds of restaurants and the only way to have a really good job in the hospitality industry is to have a recognised qualification.

And that's a tragedy of the commons. Without a commitment to train for every business that uses skilled workers, it's easier for a business to go out and pinch somebody skilled, like a skilled migrant, or someone another business has trained, than to actually invest in training. You could regulate training requirements and, say, if you employ skilled staff, you have to involve someone in the training system. You could regulate maximum hours and that would then put an emphasis on the rate of pay.

Deregulation can be a matter of life and death. The Pike River tragedy, for example, is simply a catastrophic business failure – hubris, exaggeration, ignoring warning signs, anything but a sustainable approach. Part of this comes from the profit-driven model. Business can profitably expand to include health and safety, and effects on the environment. It needs to be more cautious, careful and conservative, rather than a system favouring entrepreneurs with great visions, who talk up their share value and exaggerate things to get investment on board. Regulation would have its place there.

Take the 90-day law. A worker can be dismissed in their first 90 days, with no right of appeal. On one hand, you could debate the risk for the employer of taking on a new worker. On the other, you could acknowledge that both parties take a risk and have a rights-based approach that at least has a right of appeal.

In any case, unemployment fell hugely in the last decade *without a 90-day law* – from 161,000 in 1999 to 17,500 in 2008. The law isn't a cure for youth out of work, but a strong economy and strong labour market conditions are, even with regulation. We should remember that in many aspects of life, we are regulated all the time.

CTU response

In the face of free-market economics, we have several responses. First, we stand for people having a voice; for fair conditions of work; for the dignity of labour; for workers being treated with respect in the workplace. It's not just about pay and conditions.

Second, we're modernising, to cater to non-union workers. We've got a union called *Together*, an open organisation for people who don't fit in a current union. It's reaching out to un-unionised workers such as forestry employees.

Third, we want changes in employment law to give much greater recognition to collective bargaining rights as an important way to lift wages and conditions. The aim is to bring industry-level wages back into New Zealand over a period of time. So we have a political fight on our hands to get a sympathetic government. We're quite explicit about that. From our point of view, we're better off with a Labour-led government.

One initiative we're working on is a *sustainable development framework* – investing in public health, education and training; and the state investing in people as well as physical infrastructure.

Another initiative is the *living-wage campaign*. We all pay for low pay – poor standards of housing or underweight babies, for instance – the social costs are very significant. So caring about decent pay and conditions is not just a selfish concern of the unions; it's actually about the welfare of the community. The usual 'line' is about what the employer can afford, but our approach changes that to what people need. We want, above all, to reintroduce industry-level bargaining.

Tough, Love: Welfare in New Zealand

Sue Bradford

The welfare system in Aotearoa has been steadily undone over the last 30 years in line with government agendas aimed at maximising the ability of business to make profit – and opening our country to the full force of corporate globalisation.

Back in 1938, Labour introduced the first Social Security Act in response to the high unemployment and extreme poverty of the Great Depression. That initial framework was based on the notion that everyone had a right to a decent standard of living and that society had a collective responsibility to look after those who were unable to fend for themselves. This was followed by a revised Act in 1964, which stuck with the same principle of providing a welfare safety net.

The 1964 law is still with us, but in a much amended and degraded form. The original safety net no longer exists. Instead, successive Labour and National governments have rewritten the Act many times. Sometimes they've done this with good intent, as with the introduction of the Domestic Purposes Benefit sole parents' benefit in 1974, but more often with great damage to the wellbeing of the most vulnerable people in our society.

Welfare always needs to be considered alongside what is happening with paid work and unemployment. When National slashed benefits in 1991, they also changed employment law to weaken unions. This meant that unemployed people became even more desperate to find work, no matter how poor the pay and conditions, at the same time as the government methodically undermined the ability of workers to organise collectively.

This was a deliberate strategy aimed at making New Zealand more attractive to foreign investors, a key part of the neoliberal agenda here and around the world. Money moves to where it can make more money. The more profit that can be made, the happier the owners of capital will be.

At the same time as this was happening, the nature of paid work was shifting hugely. The same 30-year period has seen the rise and rise of what English economist Guy Standing calls the "precariat". These are people with insecure work and income who suffer from all the negative effects of economies like ours, in which high unemployment rates and punitive welfare systems work together to encourage insecurity. For more about this, Standing's book *The Precariat: The new dangerous class* is a good place to start.

In nine years of a Labour-led government, 1999–2008, nothing was done to restore the benefit levels cut by National in 1991. Steve Maharey, as Minister for Social Development, reintroduced the old 'remote areas' provision in 2004, which meant that once again whole areas of rural New Zealand became no-go zones for unemployed people. This particularly affected Māori seeking to remain in or return to their home districts. Labour abolished the Special Benefit, hugely reducing much-needed discretionary income assistance. They changed the purpose of the Social Security Act from one of meeting real needs to making getting a job the primary purpose of welfare. And they entrenched structural discrimination against the children of beneficiaries through the In Work Tax Credit component of Working For Families.

When National got back into power in 2008, they began a programme of welfare change building on the 'paid work first' approach initiated by Labour. The reforms proposed by the 2010–11 Welfare Working Group were the most significant. Commissioned by Minister Paula Bennett and led by Paula Rebstock, former chair of the Commerce Commission, the Welfare Working Group came up with a 180-page report full of recommendations on how to make Aotearoa's welfare system even harsher. Bennett's goal was to get 100,000 working-age beneficiaries out of the system within 10 years, no matter what the human cost might be.

By 2014, many of the Rebstock proposals had been implemented. Among other things, the reforms:

- introduced compulsory income management for young people on benefits, stripping them of autonomy and respect at a highly vulnerable time in their lives.
- subjected any woman on a benefit who goes on to have another child to work-testing from the time her baby turns one year old.
- gave Work and Income a role in encouraging women beneficiaries to undergo long-lasting contraception.
- extended the contracting out and privatisation of a number of Work and Income services.

- replaced unemployment, sickness and DPB benefits with one 'Jobseeker Support' category, subject to a wide range of compulsory work tests and sanctions.
- introduced a Work Ability assessment which means that many people formerly on the invalid and sickness benefits are now subject to a medical assessment which determines which kind of benefit they should be on and what kind of work they are theoretically fit for. This places huge power in the hands of designated health professionals.
- added even further sanctions to the system, including drug testing for job seekers. A first sanction means your benefit is cut by 50% for four weeks; a second sanction means it is cut altogether until you meet the 'obligation'; a third means your benefit is cancelled for 13 weeks.
- pushed welfare provision into an accrual accounting system like that applied to ACC, so that governments could scare the public with vastly exaggerated notions of how much welfare might cost in future.

All this took place during a time which saw high levels of unemployment continue, disproportionately affecting young people, Māori, Pasifika people, refugees and migrants and people living in areas like Northland, the Bay of Plenty and Te Tairawhiti. There was no government commitment to state, local government or community job creation for those most in need. As of the March 2014 Household Labour Force Survey, unemployment was running at 6%, and 254,000 people were officially jobless.

Beneficiary advocacy groups like Auckland Action Against Poverty (AAAP) see the results of the reforms coming through our doors on a daily basis. Many unemployed people simply fail to register with Work and Income because of the hurdles to help placed in their way. People who are sick, injured and disabled, including those with long-term mental health issues, suffer hugely when forced to go through work-testing and medical assessment routines. Single parents and many other beneficiaries endure a daily struggle for survival in which they plunge ever further into debt, because income support levels are not sufficient to meet even the most basic requirements for food, clothing, warmth and shelter. All this is made worse by a lack of affordable healthy housing for those on low or no incomes. Then everything gets even harder, because the government constantly reduces the supply of state housing.

Work and Income continues its slide into an ever-deepening culture of refusal, punishment and harassment, geared to keeping as many people as possible out of the benefit system. It has always been very difficult for people to advocate for themselves with the department, as the law and regulation around welfare is so complex. The benefit review and appeal system is difficult to understand and geared in Work and Income's favour. The *Child Poverty Action Group* has undertaken research which shows the negative impact of the reforms on children, for example in their report, *Benefit sanctions: Creating an invisible underclass of children?*

As I write this in mid-2014, low benefit levels, low wages, and continuing unemployment have created an ever more desperate race to the bottom, as people compete for whatever paid work exists. Once again we see the double blow that happens when welfare policy harasses and excludes beneficiaries from benefits they're entitled to, at the same time as discriminatory loans and allowances exclude increasing numbers of low income people from access to tertiary education.

Nor is the value of unpaid work in the home and community valued by government policies. Some policies make employment in the paid workforce more important to government agencies than other work which is just as valuable if not more so, such as caring for children and other dependent family members, or helping to hold together the local marae and its surrounding community.

Alternative solutions – a supportive society

Over the years, groups like ours have put a lot of work into developing alternatives and solutions to the corporate agenda on welfare and employment. The Rebstock working group provoked its own opposite – *Welfare Justice: The Alternative Welfare Working Group*. Set up by the Catholic social justice agency, Caritas, the Social Justice Commission of the Anglican Church and the Beneficiaries Advocacy Federation of New Zealand, it heard submissions from beneficiaries and communities, before writing its own report. Its findings provide useful historical and contemporary background context as well as many ideas about solutions, summarised in the group's final report *Welfare Justice for All*.

As the 2014 general election approaches, some of the key demands of Auckland Action Against Poverty include:

- Immediately repeal National's welfare reforms.
- Remove the discrimination inherent in the In Work Tax Credit.
- Implement widespread job-creation programmes in both rural and urban areas.
- Lift benefits to levels that people can live on with dignity.
- Massively speed up the supply of state housing.

UBI – Universal Basic Income

Auckland Action Against Poverty promotes a universal income paid to everyone 18 and over; to 16 & 17 year-olds living independently, with add-ons for children; to people 65+, and to those living with impairments. The UBI is also called a 'universal tax credit'.

With a UBI, the whole blame-and-shame basis of our current income support system would be gone overnight, and the associated costly, complex administration of welfare would come to an end.

UBI works with a modest amount being paid weekly to each person in their own right, with add-ons as applicable. There is no means-testing or work-testing, and no judgement is made about personal matters such as the nature of relationships.

Currently we are talking about a UBI of $14,000 p.a., with a $4000 add-on for those 65+, $4,000 for the first child and $2,000 for each subsequent child. Disability costs would be met via supplementary assistance.

A UBI would be paid for through major progressive changes in the tax system. Some current costs would be subsumed into the basic income.

Guy Standing says "Work must be rescued from jobs and labour. All forms of work should be treated with equal respect."

(For more information about this form of UBI, contact Sue Bradford or AAAP.)

- Change the culture of Work and Income so that people are treated with respect and are granted their legal entitlements as of right.
- Establish a transparent, accountable and fair review and appeal system within Work and Income.
- Reintroduce tertiary loans and allowances for all age groups, and for people on long-term benefits, with an ultimate goal of free tertiary education.
- As a first step towards legal reform, throw out the 1964 Social Security Act: start again with a new welfare law based on principle of *keeping it simple* and giving people enough to live on.
- As a second step, work towards establishing a Universal Basic Income in Aotearoa (see box).

Some of us have spent decades fighting unemployment, punitive welfare systems and poverty. We know that getting policies like these into place will only happen if other groups in the community join us in fighting for change that supports unemployed people and beneficiaries. We therefore look to NGOs, churches, unions, political parties and academics. In 2014, we fear that Labour, the largest opposition party, still doesn't seriously consider the changes we propose.

I invite anyone who supports our kaupapa to get in touch with me, with Auckland Action Against Poverty or with your local beneficiary organisation to help build our voice on these issues, for now and into the future. We have to change the story on welfare and unemployment. It is no good regretting child poverty when in fact its causes lie with the low levels of adult wages and benefits. There is endless talk about inequality at present, but talk itself will change nothing. Without organised political action which seriously changes the balance of policy and power in favour of those who have least, the neoliberal agenda on welfare and jobs will continue to cause deep damage to this and future generations.

Taking action: Auckland Action Against Poverty

Auckland Action Against Poverty was set up in 2010 as a direct action, advocacy and education group mobilising against the neoliberal agenda on jobs and welfare. It provides individual support for people facing difficulties with Work and Income. *(Find out more at www.aaap.org.nz, or contact* AAAP *at contact@aaap.org.nz)*

News Before Profits

Bill Rosenberg

In New Zealand, and internationally, news services are under stress.

Developments in technology are creating new forms of media, allowing the public more choice. Combined with discontent with the conventional media, this undermines their main income source: advertising. Meanwhile, the companies controlling our news media are increasingly focused on finances rather than news values. What's more, they are owned and run by corporate investors and executives whose skills lie in extracting more money from the business. These are mostly overseas investors who have honed these skills and have the financial backing to do it.

The main traditional alternative, public-service broadcasting, is severely weakened and under continual attack from those who see no purpose in it or who think it blocks their commercial advantage.

As a result, news values are under threat.

How did New Zealand get to this state?

The beginnings can be seen in Rupert Murdoch's takeover of the Wellington daily, the *Dominion*, in 1964, though limited by the then overseas ownership laws. It was part of a shift from family controlled to corporate newspaper ownership. During the 1980s, television broadcasting was opened up to the private television channel, TV3, and the Sky TV pay television network.[2] These developments did not have to lead to the current situation. Things could have been different if public-service broadcasting had remained strong, limits had remained on foreign and cross-media ownership, and quality had been maintained through measures such as local content requirements and limits on advertising. Instead these developments were Trojan horses for what followed.

During the late 1980s, the Lange-Douglas Government corporatised the public broadcasters into State Owned Enterprises (SOEs) with commercial objectives. Television New Zealand (TVNZ) faced competition for its advertising revenue from its private competitor, while a falling share of its income came from public funding.[3]

In 1989 broadcasting was deregulated through the Broadcasting Act 1989. There were no standards set for public-service broadcasting, no promises of funding, and no requirements for local content. There were no limits on cross-media ownership or dominance other than the weak general competition laws. A Broadcasting Commission (*NZ On Air*) was set up as the sole method of funding local content, including Radio New Zealand. The Radio Communications Act 1989 deregulated allocation of broadcasting frequencies by using an auction system intended only to ensure the government received the highest price. This could hardly have suited the newly established Sky better. The first auction, from which it was by far the biggest winner, was called only three days after the Act's passage, because Sky was "anxious for the tender to commence as soon as possible", according to an official history.[4]

Despite an environment intended to assist private broadcasting, TV3 was commercially unsuccessful and faced bankruptcy. Its receivers and Treasury lobbied to allow it to go into foreign ownership. In the meantime, Murdoch's News Corporation was itching to increase its ownership of New Zealand news media. This included wanting to buy TV2 from a government making continual threats to privatise one or both of TVNZ's channels. In 1991, the new National Government abolished all restrictions on foreign ownership of the news media other than the ineffectual conditions applying to any foreign investment.

Important features of the deregulation were then made near-impossible for future governments to change. In 1994 the government signed the General Agreement on Trade in Services (GATS), part of the new World Trade Organisation. New Zealand's exceptionally broad commitments mean that no future government may restrict overseas ownership of broadcasting nor require locally produced content.

"Toaster with pictures"

Michael Fowler, deregulatory head of the US regulator, the Federal Communications Commission under Ronald Reagan, described television as "just another appliance. It's a toaster with pictures." In other words, broadcasting was nothing more than another commodity for which 'the market' would make the best decisions for everyone. The same view was taken by the designers of New Zealand's deregulatory laws. To Treasury and other advocates of the model, audiences were 'consumers' rather than listeners, viewers or citizens. In fact the direct 'consumers' in this market are not the audience but the advertisers. MediaWorks, the owner of TV3, FOUR and RadioWorks, gets 99% of its revenue from advertising.[5]

The results

Television

In television, the repeal of controls on overseas ownership allowed Canadian media company Canwest to take control of TV3, and buy up radio stations as well to create MediaWorks. However, in 2007 it sold out to Australian investment company Ironbridge, in a debt-laden deal which in 2013, forced MediaWorks into receivership. It was rescued by a consortium of investment groups and banks.[6] The experience and motivation of such investors is financial. Ironbridge's defence against the charge that it was buying MediaWorks despite no media experience was: "Ironbridge did not know much about waste either before buying EnviroWaste."[7]

TV by dollars

Surveys showed that the outcomes of financially driven television rapidly became clear. For example, primetime TVNZ news between 1985 and 1992 showed a "marked decline in item length and a preponderance of brief sound bites". The emphasis shifted "from issues relating to politics, economics and industrial relations towards those of crime, human interest and natural disaster". Over a similar period, commercial breaks increased from 12% to 23% of the bulletin[8] and in children's programming, animated cartoons multiplied five times, replacing documentaries, news, craft, science, natural history, music, drama and Māori programmes.[9]

Local content shrank, particularly on private channels. In 1999, Canwest's TV3 and TV4 screened no new local drama or comedy shows. With pressure from the new Labour-Alliance Government and NZ On Air funding, local content increased. But in 2012, TV3 and FOUR together still broadcast less local content than either Māori Television or TV One. First-run local content fell across the seven main free-to-air channels every year from 2008 to 2012.[10] The Public Media Project estimates that in 2012, NZ On Air supported only 12.6% of first-run local content.[11]

Prime TV, established by Australia's Prime Television, was bought in 2006 by Sky. This kind of sale would be banned in many other countries because it greatly increased Sky's bargaining power in bidding for sports and other programmes. Prime is now a "showcase" to lure free-to-air viewers into subscribing to Sky, which has steadily amassed the best programmes. This creates a vicious circle of further boosting Sky's viewer numbers and buying power.

Sky was founded in 1987 by business pillars of the New Right, including wealthy supporters of Rogernomics. Murdoch's INL took control in 1997[12] but sold out in 2013. By June 2013, 49% of residential households subscribed to Sky. It has a pay television monopoly and a powerful position in television broadcasting. In other countries it would be forced to offer major sports events live to free-to-air channels. In effect, it has become the principal base for new channels, despite the attempt to provide a neutral base for digital broadcasting through non-profit Freeview.

Internet-based sports and other commercial video services will provide competition for some of Sky's offerings, but won't necessarily threaten Sky's dominance. Those are games Sky can play too, with deep pockets.

The 2013 switchover to digital broadcasting reinforced Sky's privileged position. No digital frequencies were set aside for non-commercial television, which forced regional operators to either buy access at commercial rates or cease broadcasting. Only nine of the 20 regional channels are operating on Freeview, including only three of eight non-commercial channels.[13] The leading private public-service broadcaster Stratos, and its successful non-profit associate Triangle Television (now Face TV), have in effect given up the battle and are now broadcasting solely on Sky.

Sky's dominance increasingly looks like Telecom's telephone network monopoly which led to its forced break-up. Broadcasting policy would be little different if it had been written by Sky.

The Labour-Alliance Government elected in 1999 found itself unable to do more than urge broadcasters to increase local content (with a little success). It tried to raise TVNZ's standards by imposing a public-service charter but failed because it did not fund TVNZ for the changes needed.

More successful was the creation of Māori Television and two fully funded channels on Freeview, TVNZ6 and TVNZ7. Māori Television surprised opponents with its success in becoming effectively New Zealand's only true public-service television channel. TVNZ6 and TVNZ7 drew in increasing audiences with their advertising-free children's programmes, documentaries, current affairs and full-hour news programmes but they were funded only to 2012. TVNZ closed TVNZ6 in 2011. The funding was cut in 2012 and TVNZ7 closed. The three channels had, however, shown that public-service television could attract a sizeable and loyal audience.

Radio

Radio New Zealand has demonstrated that public-service radio can attract a strong audience and respect from other media. Its National network's *Morning Report* and *Checkpoint* programmes are acknowledged news leaders, and it provides the only serious current affairs radio programmes outside volunteer-run access radio.

Two groups, The Radio Network (TRN) and RadioWorks, a MediaWorks subsidiary, dominate commercial radio, with 85% of its listening audience in 2013: 42% and 43% respectively.[14] TRN bought Radio New Zealand's extensive commercial radio network when it was privatised in 1996. It is owned by the Australian Radio Network. It in turn is owned by APN News and Media (ANM), one of New Zealand's largest newspaper owners (see below) and until February 2014, Clear Channel Communications, one of the largest and most controversial radio broadcasters in the US.[15] Both groups bought out numerous independent stations over the last two decades. They collaborate through their marketing joint venture *The Radio Bureau*, which has a near-monopoly on selling radio advertising for commercial radio. It says this is (unsurprisingly) "unique in the world".[16]

Radio for advertisers

Increasingly, network branded programming is centrally broadcast or pre-recorded, losing local content. The 'brands' are designed for advertisers rather than listeners. The Radio Bureau says each radio station brand targets "a slightly different psychographic segment of the market, which, for advertisers means little or no wastage".[17] It says New Zealand commercial radio is "arguably the most deregulated in the world".[18]

Newspapers

As in television and radio, two companies dominate newspaper publishing. Fairfax and ANM together had 90% of daily newspaper circulation in June 2013, according to Audit Bureau of Circulations data.[19]

Fairfax, part of the major Australian media empire, bought the newspaper arm of News Corporation's INL in 2003. In 2013 its newspapers had 49% of daily newspaper circulation. It owns two of the three Sunday newspapers, 10 dailies, over 60 give-away community newspapers, and over 20 magazines.

ANM took over the major newspaper publisher Wilson and Horton in 1995. Until 2012, ANM was controlled by Irish media magnate, Tony O'Reilly, through his company Independent News and Media, which still has a 17.6%

shareholding. In 2013, ANM had 41% of daily newspaper circulation, 27% of that from the *New Zealand Herald.* It owns 10 regional newspapers, including six dailies.

Media researcher Merja Myllylahti estimates that "financial institutions which don't have any inherent interest in media now hold 55.6% of ANM shares and 56.5% of Fairfax Media shares".[20] Both companies are facing falling circulation and advertising income. Circulation of Fairfax dailies fell 17% in the five years 2008–13, while ANM's fell 18% (and 27% since 2003).[21] Sharebrokers Forsyth Barr said in 1999: "the business of newspaper publishing is selling advertising",[22] yet newspaper advertising turnover fell over 30%, from $780 million in 2008 to $540 million in 2012. They have responded with outsourcing, centralising production, restructuring and staff cuts.

Alternatives

Slide to the bottom

A 2007 survey of New Zealand journalists showed it was a common experience that newsrooms had been pressured to do a story because it related to an advertiser, owner or sponsor. Over two-thirds thought commercial pressures, job losses and lack of experienced journalists, due to low pay, were compromising the media's watchdog role and investigative journalism. They were concerned about the lack of analysis and over-simplification of stories.[23]

Newspapers lost the primary role in investigative reporting to public-service television when it functioned. Public-service television barely survives. With a few notable exceptions, our top investigative journalists are no longer in newspapers or television. They are freelancers like Nicky Hager and Jon Stephenson, who too often are ignored or even scorned by our newspapers. But commercialised news media are now failing to even report the news in an informed, thorough and independent way.

There are of course alternatives such as blogs, access radio and television, citizen journalism, private non-profit public-service media, local online-only news sources such as Scoop, and thousands of international internet sources. Some do a good job of increasing opportunities for people to participate in public life, and need support for that. But they do not replace mainstream media in forming a common view of 'what matters' in the news. Nor do they draw their audience from outside their own immediate circle of interest. So they tend to weaken rather than strengthen shared understanding in the community. That lets the mainstream media set what counts as 'reality', even though it is superficial and open to political and corporate spin. The mainstream media is still needed as well as the newer alternatives – but it is not doing the job society needs.

How could it be different? According to Transparency International, "New Zealand is said to have the most deregulated media market in the Western world".[24] Few other similar countries put up with such low expectations of social responsibility and the effects of the purely profit-driven news media that is present here, let alone the dominance by just a few media companies.

We are experiencing a market failure in providing sufficient quality news, analysis and investigative journalism for a healthy society. The failure will intensify with the loss of the advertising income that subsidises news services. This increasingly urgent situation justifies regulation which addresses the failure without threatening media freedom.

Sky should be broken into a content provider and a neutral network provider which third-party channels can access at cost. All providers should be required to share coverage of sports and other events of national significance with free-to-air channels.

A specialist broadcasting authority should administer tighter rules to ensure no single commercial provider ever becomes so dominant again. New competition rules should severely limit cross-media ownership.

The government should renegotiate international commitments such as in the GATS agreement. It should introduce local content requirements for broadcasters and controls on overseas ownership of media companies that are important to the nation.

Digital frequencies should be available to not-for-profit radio and television at reduced or no cost. NZ On Air funding should be available to regional providers which meet public-service criteria.

The market failure in investigative reporting should be recognised by providing funding for such reporting to all forms of news media through an independent organisation.

Radio New Zealand should continue to be funded as New Zealand's national public-service radio. But the government should also fund a national public-service television channel and online national electronic 'newspaper' with specific responsibilities for investigative journalism.

We need much stronger protection for the independence of public funding and media organisations, to make them as free as possible from political and corporate influence. This effect comes partly from government and advertisers holding the purse strings. A ring-fenced levy such as one on all media advertising and pay television subscriptions could help fund these activities.[25] The governance of these organisations should be reviewed to ensure their boards and directors are independent and primarily have expertise in journalism and broadcasting.

1 The views expressed in this chapter are those of the author alone.

2 Smith, P. (1996). *Revolution in the air!* Auckland, New Zealand: Longman, describes this and provides a worthwhile history of the developments in television until the mid 1990s.

3 Hope, W., & Myllylahti, M. (2011). Media-communication ownership In Aotearoa-New Zealand: Legacies and contemporary trends. *Foreign Control Watchdog*, (128), 50–68.

4 Radio Spectrum Management, New Zealand Government. (2011, February 3). First auction | Radio Spectrum Management. *Radio Spectrum Management*. Retrieved January 18, 2014, from www.rsm.govt.nz/cms/customer-support/about-us/a-brief-history-of-regulation-of-radiocommunications-in-new-zealand/first-auction.

5 Vaughan, G. (2007, May 9). Ironbridge gets CanWest but happy to stay listed. *Dominion Post*, p. C1. Wellington, New Zealand.

6 Myllylahti, M. (2013). *JMAD New Zealand media ownership report 2013*. Auckland, New Zealand: AUT. Retrieved from www.aut.ac.nz/study-at-aut/study-areas/communications/profile/media-networks/journalism,-media-and-democracy-research-centre/journalists-and-projects

7 Vaughan, G. (2007). Agent for private equity in NZ. *Press*, C4.

8 Hope, W., & Myllylahti, M. (2011). Media-communication ownership in Aotearoa-New Zealand: Legacies and contemporary trends. *Foreign Control Watchdog* (128), 50–68.

9 Cocker, A. (1996). *"A toaster with pictures": The deregulation of broadcasting in New Zealand* (PhD Thesis). University of Auckland, Auckland, New Zealand. Retrieved from hdl.handle.net/2292/2026

10 Data in this paragraph from: NZ On Air. (2013). *2012 Local Content New Zealand Television*. Wellington, New Zealand: NZ On Air. Retrieved from nzonair.govt.nz/news/newspressreleases/pressrelease_2013_04_24.aspx

11 Public Media Project. (2014). *NZ TV's digital division creates a marginalised majority*. New Zealand: Public Media Project.

12 Rosenberg, B. (2008). News media ownership in New Zealand. *Campaign Against Foreign Control of Aotearoa (CAFCA)*. Retrieved from canterbury.cyberplace.org.nz/community/CAFCA/publications/Miscellaneous/mediaown.pdf

13 Public Media Project. (2014). *NZ TV's digital division creates a marginalised majority*. New Zealand: Public Media Project.

14 See www.radios.co.nz

15 Rosenberg (2008).

16 The Radio Bureau. (2006). TRB's Role. *The Radio Bureau*. Retrieved January 19, 2014, from www.trb.co.nz/standardPage_v2.asp?id=239

17 The Radio Bureau. (2006). *New Zealand radio market – Segmentation*. New Zealand: The Radio Bureau.

18 The Radio Bureau. (2006). The Radio Bureau – History of NZ Radio, NZ commercial radio history. *The Radio Bureau*. Retrieved January 18, 2014, from www.trb.co.nz/StandardPage.asp?id=180

19 See www.abc.org.nz.

20 Myllylahti (2013).

21 Calculated from Audit Bureau of Circulations data at newspaper.abc.org.nz/audit.html, various years.

22 Diversity key for media play. (1999, February 27). *Press*, p. 22. Christchurch, New Zealand

23 Hollings, J., Lealand, G., Samson, A., & Tilley, E. (2007). The big NZ journalism survey: Underpaid, under-trained, under-resourced, unsure about the future – but still idealistic. *Pacific Journalism Review*, *13*(2), 175–197.

24 Transparency International New Zealand. (2013). *Integrity Plus 2013: New Zealand National Integrity System Assessment*. Wellington, New Zealand: Transparency International New Zealand, p. 262. Retrieved from www.transparency.org.nz/2013/Integrity-Plus-2013-New-Zealand-National-Integrity-System-Assessment

25 There is a useful summary of possible public-service broadcasting models and funding mechanisms in Thompson, P. A. (2011, November 10). *Show me the money – funding possibilities for public television in New Zealand*. Presented at the 2011 SPADA Conference, Auckland, New Zealand. Retrieved from www.victoria.ac.nz/seftms/about/staff/peter-thompson/Show_Me_the_Money_Thompson-SPADA_2011.pdf

Health in an Age of Cholera

Kevin Hague

In health three models dominate our ways of seeing how illness is caused and how to prevent it. The first of these is the *biomedical*: we look for the bacteria, virus or fungus that causes the disease, or the gene that might expose an individual to it, or the chemical imbalance and so on. Historically there were debates over whether disease was spread by "microbes" or "miasma" – an invisible physical presence in the air or environment that affected those it touched. The discovery of bacteria largely ended this debate and sparked an intense focus on identifying microscopic and other biomedical causes or triggers. The actions for healing people using this model are technical in nature: chemical or other approaches to killing the microbe, righting the chemical balance, fixing the gene etc.

A second model is the *health behaviour* approach. It doesn't apply to all health conditions but, in many cases, there is a relationship between human behaviour and health outcomes. This connection follows from the landmark work of Sir Richard Doll and others in the 1950s that for the first time conclusively linked lung cancer and cigarette smoking. Tobacco, alcohol, other drugs, food, stress, sexual behaviour and many, many other aspects of 'lifestyle' are strongly linked to health outcomes. For example, smoking (which links to cancer, cardiovascular disease, diabetes and stroke) and our eating and drinking behaviours account between them for the vast majority of premature deaths in New Zealand.

With this model, if we want to take action to improve health or prevent illness, we need people to behave differently. A lot of research looks at this approach, but the basic idea is that *individuals* will make different choices about behaviour if they are provided with the right information.

This approach works well for those on the right of the political spectrum. They say "if you want to be healthier, then just make better choices." The underlying message is that if a person isn't healthy, it's their own fault.

This thinking about individual choice is so common that it's difficult to see it for what it is – ideology. We're a bit like the fish who can't see the water. In our case the 'water' is actually an economic model in which people are reduced to individual units of labour and individual consumers. One of the basic foundations of the entire standard theory of economics is that individuals will weigh up the price and quality of competing goods and make rational, self-interested choices between them. This theory has come to be applied as fact not only in economics but much more widely.

However, any examination of what actually occurs in real world markets shows that people seldom behave as the theory predicts, even in economics. When the theory is applied in other spheres, it becomes even less helpful. In health, if the theory held, we should expect to see illnesses spread out fairly evenly across New Zealand. The reasoning is that every community would have some members who are great at making choices and some who are poor at it, and everything in between.

But this is not what we actually observe. In fact nearly every disease is strongly concentrated in particular population groups, so something very different is going on. When we look at the particular population groups who have high concentrations of illness, it will be no surprise to find that they are groups who are in some way marginalised – Māori, poor people, Pasifika communities, refugees and other predictable groups. The more marginalised a community is, the worse its health is likely to be.

This leads to the third model for health, where the 'cause' of ill health is a *risk environment* (sometimes called 'social determinants'). This approach still accepts that biology can contribute to ill health. But it says that biology by itself is insufficient, because factors like poverty or discrimination can put people 'in harm's way'. Likewise, individual behaviour plays a part, but doesn't necessarily result from rational decisions. Few people looking at their own behaviour around eating, drinking, sex and so on would claim to be consistently rational decision-makers (try it now!), and research overwhelmingly supports that conclusion.

Those risk environments tilt the 'playing field'. A person standing in the middle of a field can move in any direction with equal ease. But when the field becomes tilted, some directions become easier, and some harder. Risk environments push people toward unhealthy behaviours, and also undermine any sense of control. Risk environments such as poverty create risk factors, such as low self-esteem, which limit people's choices.

The approach we take to improve health is health promotion. It's all about societies tackling risk environments by combating issues like poverty and racism, enabling both communities and the people within them to have the same sense of control over their lives that more privileged communities currently enjoy.

These processes are political, based on understanding how power in society shapes outcomes and the social interactions between people. This approach is very different from the right-wing formula of individual liberty and unconstrained rational choice.

We constantly observe that a great deal of health is shaped by factors outside the health sector. If we want to improve health, we can have the biggest impact by breaking down those risk environments. But New Zealand's current (right-wing) government has drastically reduced investment in health promotion.

Many would argue that ensuring that citizens are as healthy as they can be is a core part of our collective duty to each other, which we express through the state. Preventing illness through health promotion programmes is something we expect from governments. So is the provision of health services that are intended to cure us, mend us or make us feel better, when we become sick or injured.

It is sometimes useful to consider what an outsider would make of the present-day arrangements that we may find hard to 'see' because we are acclimatised to them. In New Zealand some health services are provided by the public sector, and some by the private sector. Some services are publicly funded, while others must be paid for privately. Would someone observing this pattern for the first time be able to figure out the logic and reasoning behind it?

The answer is surely no. If I go to see a GP (in most parts of the country) the service will be provided by someone in the private sector. I will privately pay a fee but most of the cost will be publicly funded. If I go to see a dentist, however, the service will be privately provided and I will have to pay the full cost myself. By contrast, a medical specialist service will be both funded and provided publicly through the public health system. There is no logic behind this; it is all mostly the result of historical accident. The 'line' between the public and private sectors varies service by service.

Over the years, different governments have moved the line more towards the public end or the private end, depending on their political beliefs. Under the 1999–2008 Labour-led governments, for example, there was considerable investment in increasing the public funding of General Practice services, on the condition that patient fees were reduced or held steady. This effectively grew the public portion of the health pie, while the private portion shrank.

The National-led governments since 2008 have had a belief in greater individual self-reliance and less mutual responsibility for each other's welfare. They believe that the state should be smaller and so have begun to reduce the public portion of health. This happens with the active encouragement of some parts of the private sector, who see the possibility of making money from privatising healthcare, and reducing it to other service offers, such as hairdressing or window cleaning.

One way in which this has occurred is through the increase in the private provision of services. District health boards have been encouraged to contract out some of their elective surgery workloads to the private sector, for example. Where new hospitals or healthcare facilities are required, the Government increasingly insists that there should be private sector capital to fund such projects. The claim is that the private sector is more efficient. The reality is often that funders need to cover a profit margin *in addition to* the cost of providing the services themselves. In other words, it costs more. Such privatisation is driven by political positions and needs, not practical or economic ones.

Government has also been shrinking the public portion of health by putting less money in. It's true that year on year, the dollar amount of the Government's Health budget has increased. But it hasn't increased as fast as is needed for health services. That has left many health services either really stretched or completely unable to continue. Where service users need to pay a fee themselves, it has generally been increasing, putting those services increasingly beyond the reach of the poorest New Zealanders. At the other end of the wealth scale, if publicly funded services are further unavailable or their quality is eroded by underfunding, those who can afford to do so can seek private health insurance.

Overall, as the Government has shrunk the size of the state in the health sector, access to health care has become harder for those who are at greatest risk and already have the poorest health. Quite rapidly now, New Zealand is moving towards a radically uneven distribution of both health and health services. If we are unsure where this will take us, we need only look across the Pacific to the United States, where the most extreme inequality in the provision of health care is evident.

New Zealand has just celebrated the 75th anniversary of Michael Joseph Savage's Social Security Act. Here are the planned objectives laid out at that time for the public health system:

- Health care should be a fundamental right for all New Zealanders.
- There should be no access barriers, certainly not financial ones.

- Services should be universally available.
- Services should be preventive in focus.
- Services should be integrated.

Most people hearing these slogans nod their heads in agreement and assume they must be a modern formulation! This emphasises for me that the values framing the welfare state are as relevant now as they were in 1938 – collective responsibility for each other and the universal right to good lives. And these values are worth fighting for.

We need to elect governments and district health boards who will fight for three goals:

- focus on the values of Savage's Social Security Act.
- empower marginalised people.
- create physical, social and economic environments that will promote health.

We need to engage New Zealanders in the necessary conversations about how decisions should be made in health. And we need to ensure that the health and wellbeing of New Zealanders is seen as a higher priority than, say, tax cuts for the most wealthy, or faster motorway trips.

Rogered by Rogernomics

Tim Hazledine

Pundits have placed New Zealand's Rogernomics episode as a 'textbook' example of economic reform, but in fact it is more interesting than that. Most textbooks – for sure, most Economics textbooks – make terribly dull reading, in part because they stick doggedly to the safe path of conventional wisdom, avoiding anything controversial or innovative.

That's probably how it should be. It would be irresponsible of us to impregnate the impressionable minds of young students with wild new ideas and unproved theories. And even now, three decades after the 1984–91 'reform' regime got underway, the unproved theory that underpinned Rogernomics occupies, at most, no more than a chapter in introductory Economics texts.

You might be surprised by this, especially if you've actually waded through one of these textbooks, at school or university. Isn't economics all about free markets and competition and maximising profits and so on? Isn't this the essence of the capitalism that Roger Douglas and his sidekicks forced onto the regulated, controlled, inefficient planned economy they inherited from Robert Muldoon? Well, actually, no. Both the before and the after of this view of our history are over-simplified to the point of gross distortion. Take the politics of it first. Here there is really no difference at all between Rob and Rog. They were both arrogant, dogmatic bullies who had no compunction about taking full advantage of New Zealand's uniquely one-chamber 'elected dictator' political system to ram through their wilful schemes, riding roughshod over – admittedly rather feeble – opposition.

Both were very interested in the economy, if not in economics as a discipline. Muldoon took over the Finance portfolio, in a dangerous pairing with the premiership. Douglas only needed to be Minister of Finance, because his nominal boss David Lange was a whimsical man, bored by economics, content to let the 'Rogernomes' do their thing until it was too late to stop them.

What about the substance of their economic policies? Muldoon is remembered now for his pig-headed mishandling of our exchange rate and for the dreadful Think Big megaprojects. These were errors, though well meant, whose folly was, however, exaggerated by Roger Douglas. He wanted to provide political cover for his own radical intrusions into the fabric of the economy under the guise of emergency action needed to resuscitate an economic basket-case – the "Albania of the South Pacific".

The facts are quite different. The New Zealand of the early 1980s was already – and had been for a century – a fully functioning capitalist market economy. We had a smooth-running stock exchange, secure property rights, an efficient and honest civil service and judiciary, a trusting and trustworthy culture – all the things you need to go to the market with. Under this system our farmers and factories had built up the great primary export industries that paid our way – very well – in the world. One of our many home-grown business enterprises – Glaxo – had exported itself to become – by this time – the largest manufacturing company in Britain. In the Holyoake-Kirk-Muldoon era our workers, government and industries had responded to the loss of fair access to the then crucial British market with a remarkably successful process of diversifying exports, which continues to this day. Muldoon had delivered many genuine reforms – social and economic. He had negotiated with a reluctant Australian administration a Closer Economic Relations (CER) treaty, that still stands out internationally amongst such arrangements, in particular because it guarantees free mobility of workers between our countries. Can you imagine a US President ever signing a treaty with this property?

Muldoon had abolished the railway's monopoly over long- and medium-distance freight haulage. And he abolished another monopoly – compulsory unionism, under the shelter of which (as always happens with protected monopolies) the trade union movement had become slack and timid. The weakness of the labour unions would be sadly demonstrated just a few years later with their shameful capitulation to the union-breaking Employment Contracts Act (ECA), which resulted in a halving of union membership over just three years in the early 1990s.

You may or may or not agree with the substance of these reforms. But they can hardly be credited as the work of a Communist dictator, *qua* Albania. The fact is that, with or without Rob Muldoon, the New Zealand hijacked by the zealots of Rogernomics was a country on the path of social and economic liberalisation. There was no economic necessity – there rarely is – for a revolution.

So what happened? What were the economic consequences of Rogernomics? In one word: terrible. I cannot find an example of any developed economy in modern times that has inflicted such harm upon itself. It is true that greater damage would be done just a few years later to the economies of the former Soviet Union and its satellites, in which the sudden collapse of socialist central planning resulted in many cases of a virtual halving of GDP, from already depressed levels. However, these were societies in which the citizens by 1990 had almost no memory of living in a mixed private–public social democratic system. They quite literally did not know how to behave in the market economy, and it has taken a couple of decades for them to learn how to play this game.

New Zealand, as I have said, was a different case – a stable little capitalist state, courageously fighting its corner in the big tough world economy. But the blows from within rained down – 104 major 'reforms' pummeling the body-economic. Too much to take. One manufacturing job in three was lost, and with those jobs basically went the blue-collar core that is crucial to the chances of less skilled workers being able to support their families in decency. Unemployment tripled between 1984 and 1991, to 11% or more (depending how you measure it) – our worst post-war recession, even including the most recent 2008–9 dip imported from the Global Financial Crisis.

After the tsunami of reform had receded, our economy slowly picked up the pieces and rebuilt itself through the 1990s, though the recovery has always been exaggerated by reform apologists. They use the old statistical trick of timing economic growth beginning at the very trough of deep recession, in 1992, ignoring the fact that this recession had itself been caused by the policy revolution. In any case, such economic growth as did occur was largely enjoyed by the upper-income group, with little or no improvement in the living standards of lower and middle income households – culminating in New Zealand showing the largest increase in inequality of any OECD economy from 1985 to 2000. Most noticeably, perhaps, an income gap between New Zealand and Australia, which had first appeared in the late Muldoon era, ballooned out to around 30% or more, and has never been pulled back.

So what went wrong? This is where the non-textbook thing comes in. To a remarkable extent the 104 major reforms were based on the same, simple idea – an *avant garde* doctrine called Agency Theory. Here all economic – and indeed most social – life is seen as a series of interactions between two people: someone who wants something done (the 'principal') and someone who is able to do it (the 'agent'). It is assumed that everyone is concerned solely with maximising their own selfish interests, that they will have no scruples about how they achieve this, and that they are fully competent to figure out how to do this – self-interested, opportunistic, rational, in the economic jargon. I call this the 'selfish shit' model, for short.

Because the principal's and the agent's interests are unlikely to coincide naturally, the latter must be brought into line somehow. There are basically two ways the principal can achieve this: by threats, or by bribes. Threats were deployed at both ends of the labour market. High unemployment and the demoralising ECA were used to cow workers into line, whilst the fire-sale mass privatisations of public enterprises were justified by claiming (quite falsely as it turned out) that management and directors would be 'disciplined' to perform well by the threat of a stock market takeover.

However, just in case that didn't work, the top managers were given bribes as well – bonuses and rights to buy shares themselves at below-market prices. The resulting inflation of CEO remuneration (here and in other English-speaking countries) was of course responsible for much of the blow-out in income inequality, along with the squeeze on worker wages.

So what is wrong with Agency Theory, and why has it indeed never made it into the mainstream of reputable Economics textbooks? Three things. First, it stinks, morally, with its abnegation of all concepts of honour, decency, generosity, duty, pride in doing a good job. Second, it is factually wrong in this respect, thank goodness. But, third, it has the insidious effect of self-validation – if you persistently mistrust people, then eventually some at least will say: "If you are going to assume I am out to cheat you all the time, then, to heck with it, I will." And there go the invisible, unenforceable bonds of trust and goodwill that make civilization possible. This truly is not good economics, and it is really just as well that those mainstream Economics textbooks give no more than a chapter to Agency Theory and its applications.

But somehow the word hasn't got around about the unfortunate consequences of applying the theory to real people living in a real economy. Over and over, people who know nothing about this country refer to the "success" of our "reforms". Worse, people who should know better do it too. The most persistent offender is probably the British weekly news magazine *The Economist*, which has been talking up Rogernomics for more than two decades. In October 2000 their Economics Editor, Pam Woodall, came out to see for herself. She scheduled about three days of meetings in Wellington, to be followed by a similar programme in Auckland, including a meeting with me. But, a day before this, Ms Woodall contacted me to say that she had found out all she needed to know from the good folk in Wellington (Treasury, Business Roundtable *et al.*), and was scrapping the Auckland part of her trip to return at once to London. No need to talk to the people actually affected by the reforms; nor to loony left-wing profs, as she no doubt had been briefed. I offered to go out to Auckland airport to meet her in transit, and she reluctantly agreed to this, but our brief chat was clearly a waste of time for both of us. In due course her piece turned up in *The Economist:* 'Can the Kiwi economy fly?' (December 2, 2000). This article made most of the mistakes I have listed above. I wrote a letter in protest. I said that "New Zealand had created a level playing field, but nobody had turned up to play" – a snappy little line which earned me prime place on the letter page (December 9, 2000).

The misinformation or just intellectual laziness goes on and on. Most recently, our Productivity Commission – a right-wing government policy research agency – arranged for three economists from the OECD in Paris (the 'rich countries' club') to write a report on New Zealand's "productivity paradox" – the puzzle of our mediocre economic performance, despite having "growth-friendly structural policy settings".[1] This is code for the captain of the ship of state setting a course for laissez-faire monetarism, and then going below and letting the ship or economy sort things out for itself. Well, perhaps those policy settings actually aren't so growth-friendly, at least not when carried to extremes, as in New Zealand under Rogernomics. The authors sum up: "The set of reforms [was] successful in stemming the relative economic decline, but has failed to put the country on a clear convergence path" with the rest of the OECD.

Well, indeed it hasn't. Note that – typically for a work like this – the Productivity Commission paper (which is really about interesting things like innovation and intellectual property) gives no actual evidence that Rogernomics ever did stem relative decline. It's just assumed that it must have, because that's what the theory says should happen. A genuinely open-minded analysis would be more likely to link poor performance to poor 'policy settings' and look elsewhere – even to our closest neighbour, Australia – for a more moderate, Keynesian, mixed-economy alternative.

1 An International Perspective on the New Zealand Productivity Paradox. New Zealand Productivity Commission WP 2014/1, April 2014.

Cool, Clear Water

Mike Joy

This chapter is based on an interview with freshwater scientist Mike Joy. He explains how free market-based economics have allowed dairy farms to seriously damage our rivers and lakes.

I want to talk about the quality of water in New Zealand, and that will take us to the business agenda for water management.

Fresh water is top of the list of essentials for New Zealanders. From a Māori perspective, water is crucial to life. Our lakes and rivers are at the heart of New Zealand's lifestyle – fishing, swimming, tourism – and groundwater is crucial for drinking.

But intensive dairying means water is critical and that raises questions of its quality and how to protect it – which was supposed to be the role of the Resource Management Act (RMA).

Government has failed to bring in any national policies, so in that vacuum you have 16 regional councils basically doing their own thing. They are subject to influence from the farming industry and have chosen to ignore the main impact of dairying, which is 'diffuse nutrient pollution'.

The problem of diffuse nutrient pollution is that nitrogen, mainly from cows' urine, travels through the soil and into waterways. There's so much of it, and as the cow urinates in one small spot, before plants can take it up, it's moved through the soil past the roots and then sideways into rivers and lakes and down into groundwater. But government has focused just on dairy shed waste, which is only a small proportion of the pollution, around 10 to 15%. So whenever you hear about compliance, they're talking only about dairy sheds. The only way to control nitrogen pollution under the RMA is to require consent for intensive dairying – which government chooses not to do.

The other big issue is sediment, which comes mainly from forest clearance. In the 1970s government legislated so-called 'sheep retention schemes' that paid farmers to clear forest and make more 'productive land' – even though the farmers knew full well that it was crazy, because the soil was going to disappear. And it did. Erosion caused the loss of the forest protecting the soil on the hillside.

This took place when we lost our special status with Britain, because it joined the European Union. Profits dropped sharply, with lowered commodity prices, and farmers were left surviving on government subsidies to clear land. They cleared land that they never would have previously, with one significant result. All of that sediment coming down our rivers now causes a huge problem of flood control, ecological impact and the choking of estuaries and harbours. The ongoing effects require very costly remedies, with stop-banking and other flood controls. And that's just one example of government intervention that has led to heavy environmental impacts that we're only just beginning to see now.

All this means water gets degraded. One way water quality is measured is by how much available oxygen varies in the water. The more it fluctuates over a 24-hour period, the worse it is. In a natural pristine river, there's very little change in oxygen over 24 hours. But more nutrients in water leads to more plant growth, and the result is algal and weed blooms. More algae means more plant respiration, so more extreme oxygen fluctuation, because plants take up oxygen during the day and respire at night.

This happens with the Manawatu River. At the Hopelands Road monitoring site below a predominantly dairy catchment, it goes from a low of 40% dissolved oxygen at three or four in the morning up to a supersaturated 160% at three or four in the afternoon. At both ends of that scale, it kills the fish and most of the life. Unless the fish can gulp air at the surface, as goldfish do, they're dead.

There's a world-wide calculation for this fluctuation: a score of 0–3 is considered a healthy river; 3–6 is satisfactory; anything higher than 6 is degraded. At two sites, the Manawatu River measured 107, the highest anywhere in the world. The Cawthron Institute in Nelson has pulled 570 measurements from round the world: not one of them was anywhere near that. The highest was around 80 in Belgium, from below a wastewater treatment plant on a rather sick river.

Planting up the stream banks and getting the cows out of the water will help make the streams healthier, but

From an economic point of view, one kilogram of nitrogen will pollute 88,500 litres or 88 cubic metres of water (will take it from pure water to exceeding nitrate limit (11.3 mg/l) for drinking water).

The average dairy farm is leaching around 30–40 kg per hectare per year.

Then it costs between 50c and a dollar a cubic metre to return it to drinkable standard again using a treatment plant – in other words, many times the profit the farmer has made in milk production.

it won't stop the nitrogen, which gets there through the soil profile, not overland. There are two main solutions. One, only let the cows out for a few hours to feed on the grass and then onto a concrete pad to collect the urine, which can halve the nitrogen leached. Two, stop putting nitrogen fertiliser onto the land, which means less of it leaching down through the soil.

The real culprit is farming intensity. There are two examples where controls were placed on cow numbers: Lake Taupo because it's so iconic, and the Manawatu. In both cases Federated Farmers fought hard against it. In the Manawatu case, Federated Farmers and Fonterra fought it all the way to the High Court. It's been upheld, in fact strengthened, and the plan has been enacted, but after all that, the staff were told not to apply it.

Yet there are some very progressive farmers who see the public reaction to water quality deterioration and are changing their farming practices. Economists can show that less intensive farming equals more profit – a rise from 4% average return on investment to 12 or 13%. Their inputs are way less than the others and so are their costs and ecological impacts. Some are on once-a-day milking, they are all using less fertiliser, have fewer cows, less overhead, and their profitability is much higher.

Meanwhile, dairy land prices have been going up and up for two decades. It's just a free-for-all, with no cost on pollution, thus the land prices are based on the expectation that there will be no cost on pollution. So our land is now five times more expensive than land with equivalent production in Australia. Everything is more expensive in New Zealand, so when you're competing to make the cheapest commodity, milk powder – our biggest seller – we've become one of the dearest places to produce it.

Mismanaging the market

The individual family farm is quite rare now. Agri-business, the corporatisation and industrialisation of farming, is happening in a big way, e.g., in Southland and Canterbury. And that brings us to the Canterbury Water Management Strategy. The democratically elected council had a number of people who were making a really intense effort to protect the waters of Canterbury, opposing the big irrigation developments that the National Government wanted. So that government removed the elected Canterbury Regional Councillors and put their own people in as decision-makers.

Previously, we didn't have any limits on nitrogen in water. We had guidelines at .44 mg per litre, or .44 parts per million. That was considered safe to protect the freshwater ecosystem. The Manawatu River was getting up to around one or two milligrams per litre. Now the limit in Canterbury is around six. In the new National

Policy Statement, the bottom line in the National Objectives Framework is around 6–7 mg per litre, which is higher than almost anywhere in the OECD.

For context elsewhere in the world, the bottom of the Yangtze River in China is around 3 or 4 mg per litre. The highest in the OECD is the Thames, above 6 mg. And off the coast of the Mississippi River, there's a dead zone the size of Europe, because of nutrient run-off. Here, following the Canterbury Plan, the level of nitrogen could rise in the National Policy Statement to higher than China, the Thames and the Mississippi.

Using Canterbury as a regional model for the nation, the new nitrogen limits are clearly about giving headroom for dairy expansion. But the one thing that can't be mitigated is nitrogen, except through expensive feed pads and housing cows. So the question is, when is it toxic to life and to us? The problem is that long before it becomes toxic, other drastic effects have already kicked in – the nutrient spawns algae growth that causes the changes in oxygen. We're moving from a safe level to one that is completely unsafe.

It's the same thing with the Ruataniwha Dam in Hawke's Bay, where government is quite clearly involved. Government obviously sees this as setting a precedent. If they can do Ruataniwha, then it will be the precedent for the rest of the country.

So the dam proponents have come up with a scam called 'Single Nutrient Limitation'. They say plants need both phosphorus and nitrogen to grow and they propose that we control the phosphorus. Therefore we don't have to worry how high the nitrogen gets, until it gets to toxic levels. This is correct in theory and in test tubes, but in reality, the science and worldwide experience is quite clear – you can't control the phosphorus. You can't stop it coming out of the hill country. You can't stop what's already there in the sediment from 100 years of farming. There are any number of new studies from all over the world where attempts have been made to control phosphorus that haven't worked.

In a real sense, what's happening with these irrigation schemes is the privatisation of water. You're taking something that belongs to everybody – the water flowing down the rivers – you're extracting it, then selling it back to people. But from a farming point of view, as the hearings show, water from the Ruataniwha will be so expensive that it won't be worthwhile farming. It's about a group of people owning that water, the Hawke's Bay Regional Investment Company Limited (HBRIC Ltd), and selling it to other people. Yet the money for HBRIC comes from ratepayers and investors.

The attraction for farmers is that sheep and beef property is worth maybe $5,000–10,000 a hectare. But if a farmer irrigates, then converts to a

The other extreme is sheep farming, which produces around 2kg of nitrogen per hectare per year, versus at least 20kg on a dairy farm, but more like 40kg and up to 130kg on irrigated farms.

So the profit on sheep farming is a bit less but the impacts are way less.

In effect we're subsidising the most intensive type of farming – dairy.

dairy farm, suddenly the land is worth $30,000 a hectare. So there's a one-off set of winners who walk away with the capital gain from the land, but the farming itself is not going to make any money.

That's within New Zealand. Now, globally, there'll be an increase in demand. But our production increases are being outstripped all over the world, and often by Kiwi farmers and Fonterra setting up in China and in South America. In a few years China has gone from producing much less than we do to producing way more than we do. The projection is that selling will become a problem for us.

Who owns water?

According to John Key, nobody owns water. But clearly the value of the farms in Canterbury is their water allowance. And if you look at hydro-electricity production, water has a massive value.

Take the Genesis power scheme on the Central Volcanic Plateau. It was a New Zealand Government power scheme, but the Tongariro power development takes water from the Whanganui River, the Rangitikei and others, then diverts it to Lake Taupo, and on down the Waikato River, producing electricity the whole way down.

For the people of the land, it was their waters that were cut off. When it was done for the good of New Zealand, in a non-profit situation, that was possibly more acceptable. But when a private corporate takes our rain and ruins our rivers, to sell electricity to us at a profit, then it's totally different. The iwi there, Tuwharetoa and Ngati Rangi, they just feel they've been totally tricked.

At least, if you use water for hydro-electricity, it's going back in a similar condition to what you took out. But in an irrigation scheme, you're taking it out pure, you're putting it onto a farm, taking all those nutrients with it, and going back into the river, in a much worse state than originally.

This conflicts directly with Māori values of water and its spiritual importance. Māori have great problems with pouring pollution into rivers. Now, there is some hope in co-management, as in the Waikato. One of the key goals of the Waikato Tainui Act of Parliament is to improve the state of the water, so it will be swimmable and fishable over its entire length. But to achieve that would mean major changes to land use there.

It's very much like the National Policy Statement changes, where the bottom-lines will allow things to get a whole lot worse. There's no match between the technical description and the rhetoric. The Executive Summary of the technical reports says one thing and the body of the document says the other. They claim they're preserving fresh water, but in fact it's the opposite.

A case in point is the Land and Water Forum which talked about collaboration but was simply a compromise, weighted 95% towards industry and 'stakeholders' – power companies and farming. To me, all New Zealanders are stakeholders.

The zone committee in Canterbury is a really good example of how they failed. They say the only way you can have current farming is for the *public* to compromise: you have to accept degradation of our waterways. To me that's blackmail.

What must be done?

If we started valuing things other than GDP, it would be obvious we're destroying the natural world to prop up the economic one. One councillor said at a talk I gave: "You want a whole lot of money to set up a wastewater treatment plant or to reduce farming like in the Taupo situation: $95m would pay half a dozen farmers to cut back on their farms to protect the lake. That's a huge debt on the future of our children."

But I think if we don't have the economic debt, then we have an *ecological* debt. I'd much rather be in hock to a bank than to the environment. Banks can go broke, you can tell them to go away or you can write off loans. But you can't fix ruined rivers and lakes and polluted groundwater. They are the legacy we're leaving.

There's one other legacy, and that's soil contaminated with cadmium. It comes from intensive farming applying huge amounts of superphosphate onto soil. It's all about maximising production without thinking about the cost of it.

So I'd propose three responses.

First, a capital gains tax, because capital gains are driving the intensification of farming, and the rise in value of the land.

Second, a price on nutrient loss, which could mean measuring nitrogen loss, so you would then have something to retain. You would maximise production while minimising your loss of nitrogen to the environment.

Third, a cap on dairying. We've already gone too far, but at least we should stop right here. Even if we stop tomorrow, things will still get worse for decades, because we have this legacy now.

There has to be public pressure. We've got a government with a long-stated ideology that more farming is better and more intensification is better. But when the sums are done, there's nothing to back it up.

Charter Schools

John O'Neill

I hope readers will forgive the rather intemperate tone of this chapter. Usually, I try to write reasonably balanced analyses of educational issues, recognising that education is complex and that there are often multiple possible policy solutions to 'wicked' educational problems. But, the whole debate about charter schools is simply infuriating. From everything I have read about their real effects overseas during the last 20 years (as opposed to their promised effects), it seems to me that they are no more than the educational equivalent of 19th-century snake-oil elixirs, or the health supplements industry of today. The evidence for the benefits of charter schooling is highly questionable but it is marketed, or peddled, very cleverly indeed. So, just for once, I want to write about charter schools without having to try and be fair to the assertions of their advocates. I need to vent some of the utter frustration I and others feel whenever politicians and officials glibly state that their education policy decisions are based on evidence – but the only evidence they choose to use is information that justifies the policy option that has already been chosen in advance.

In the 1990s, 2000s and 2010s, charter, or free schools have been established in various countries around the world as an alternative to state schools. Populist politicians, neoliberal think tanks, corporations and the super-wealthy individuals who set out to shape public policy under the pretext of 'charity', justify their introduction on the basis that the public school system has supposedly failed children and families for decades. They claim that as a result, there is a crisis in public schooling, which only the private sector can solve on behalf of government and the taxpayer. This is, essentially, a manufactured crisis. The overriding purpose is to enable systematic transfer of public funding for education to the private sector.

Along the way, these charter supporters may forge tactical political alliances with (and offer cosmetic concessions to) disadvantaged cultural, ethnic, religious or other minorities. But the ideological agenda, the *privatisation of the state education system*, remains the larger goal.

Charter schools get state funding but operate under a contract with for-profit companies or not-for-profit charitable trusts, or groups of parents. They are controversial because their classroom methods are frequently authoritarian. Their academic results are very mixed. And their claims to innovation in teaching, learning and curriculum often do not bear close scrutiny. They typically set up in areas of high poverty and social disadvantage. The contract for running the charter school is signed by the government and the private organisation, not the government and the local community. The evidence from overseas is that charter schools often arrive in local communities, or public schools are converted into charter schools, against the express wishes of the local community. So, quite apart from privatising the public funding that goes to charter schools, it is also a calculated way of setting aside local democratic rights.

It is a bitter irony that high poverty and social disadvantage are the combined result of two factors: a long-term failure of government to invest in communities; and the more recent freedom for global corporations and wealthy individuals to avoid paying taxes. Yet, charter schools are sold to these same poor and marginalised communities as governments and the private sector working on their behalf in a Public Private Partnership (PPP).

The official purpose of charter schools is to deliver tailor-made teaching and curriculums to poor children to ensure that more of them meet expected norms of achievement, attendance and behaviour. The evidence from overseas is that while some charter schools produce good academic results for some children, they do not do so for all children who attend. Often the most disadvantaged either don't get entry or are discarded by charter schools. They then have no option but to return to a local community school. Another sad irony is that politicians and better-off families who advocate 'no excuses' military discipline and curriculum gruel for the children of the poor would not accept the same deal for their own children.

Since the mid-20th century, the state in New Zealand has funded and provided universal compulsory schooling at primary and secondary levels. Until recently, this held true, irrespective of whether Labour or National was in government. Schooling was generally understood as a public good in the sense that it helped to build and maintain the social fabric, advance local, regional and national economic productivity and encourage active citizenship within a social democracy.

Because education provides these considerable public benefits, it was understood during these decades that the state should pay for schooling, and do so through progressive general taxation of income. Taxation was regarded as an equitable form of economic and social redistribution, to ensure that everyone had sufficient access to basic public services for their needs.

Through health, welfare, social security and education, the state could attempt to compensate for the worst effects of the genetic lottery, as well as variable access to market information and poverty that lasts from one generation to the next. Moreover, the state accepted a moral obligation to do so.

Since the 1980s, things have changed, gradually at first, but now with increasingly one-sided zealotry. The New Zealand Parliament passed legislation for the introduction of a new system of charter schools in 2012 (to be called Partnership Schools or Kura Hourua). Ironically, though, New Zealand already had charter schools – more than 2,500 of them. Here's what happened.

The 1989 Education Act preserved the notion of schooling as a public good. This was to take place through an agreement, or 'charter', between the Crown and the local community. Funding was to be allocated transparently for use according to the priorities decided by the local community, based on balanced assessments of the needs of students and the community.

The 1989 Education Act was also designed to be highly flexible. It provided for groups of parents in a local community to apply to the Minister of Education to establish a special character school or kura kaupapa Māori in cases where existing state schooling could not meet local community needs. These too would be fully funded and fully provided state schools, subject to the same policies and regulations as any other state school. In making a decision, moreover, the Act required the Minister to evaluate the effects of establishing the proposed school on the community as a whole.

Ever since 1989, politicians and bureaucrats have carefully whittled away at the social democratic elements of the charter. It is now little more than a contract between an increasingly powerful state machinery and an almost powerless local community board of trustees. In this sense, governments and officials in New Zealand have spent the last quarter century actively eroding the social democratic principles of the public school charter.

The original purpose of the school charter was to document an agreement between partners, with an equal mix of local community and national system goals. The process was to be mediated by an even-handed Education Review Office (ERO) and a Parent Advocacy Council. This kind of charter was never really given a chance to work. Instead, the demands of the Crown partner steadily increased. National Education Goals and National Administration Guidelines smothered local community aspiration, creativity and need. The

ERO became government's watchdog, for many years undertaking audits of systems rather than evaluations of learning. To this day it sees its role to ensure that boards of trustees implement government policy unquestioningly.

Instead of social democracy at the local school community level, we have New Public Management (the ideology that public services must be managed like private businesses) run riot. The audit culture imposed on schools for 25 years has not worked. The deliberate erosion of trust within school communities and between teachers and trustees has proven toxic. Teachers and trustees are blamed for not properly doing the jobs that the state demands when, in fact, it is the ideologically driven actions of politicians and officials that need to be held to account.

In a way it is puzzling that the National-led government has chosen the controversial charter school route, when it was quietly leaching increasing amounts of public funding to the families of privately educated children anyway. Look at how they do it.

Since 2008, the government has significantly increased the public subsidy paid to children who attend private schools, and the number of scholarships to permit state school children to attend them. It has also enabled financially struggling independent schools to become 'integrated' into the state school system, while the independent schools continue to charge several thousand dollars each year in attendance dues.

The government's logic has been that it is 'inequitable' to pay different education subsidies to families attending private vs public schools.

On this argument, all families are equally deserving, irrespective of their particular financial circumstances and their children's life chances. This logic is perverse. It completely abandons traditional social democratic principles – the idea that education is a public good and that its purpose is to redistribute educational opportunities, not reinforce educational inequalities.

The National Government has already argued that holding 51% of state assets still constitutes a public ownership model. On this argument, it can justify establishing a further 1,245 or so charter schools, whether or not their local communities want them. As the American, English and Swedish models have shown over more than two decades, there is precious little research evidence that these schools work. Where they do, it tends to be only for the more motivated, organised and committed of disadvantaged families.

In New Zealand it is regarded as politically acceptable that a quarter of children are living in poverty in 2013. It is also now regarded as politically acceptable to fob these children and their families off with the education policy solution of charter schools. Yet 20 years after their introduction overseas, we still have no reliable evidence that charter schools help to change the financial and social circumstances that have been determined for poor children and their families by powerful political and business interests.

Charter schools will do little or nothing for New Zealand children and families in poverty. But they will create plenty of profit and other forms of capital for their operators. Can communities resist and, if so, how?

There are, thankfully, examples of courageous school communities who have challenged the political and bureaucratic standover tactics that are used to impose charter schools against the wishes of families. In Aotearoa, the recent experiences of schooling reorganisation in Christchurch and in the special school sector have been encouraging. They show that it is possible to stand up to the Minister and the Ministry, provided that parents and community groups organise themselves to do so.

Specifically with respect to charter schools, the experience of organised resistance by the Downhills school local community in London shows how easy it is, on one level, to challenge the lies that politicians and officials use in order to manufacture the crisis that they need to justify replacing local democratic governance with a private commercial contract. (www.academiesandlies.org.uk)

On another level, the Downhills community experience also shows the extreme lengths to which politicians, aided and abetted by officials and private organisations, will go in order to implement an unproven educational ideology. To the extent that Downhills parents, trustees and teachers have been able to resist a government imposed agenda, they have succeeded by: (i) challenging the slick truth claims of politicians, officials and charter school operators; (ii) seeking alliances with researchers and other groups of parents in similar circumstances to counter official misinformation campaigns; and (iii) engage their own parent community fully in information sharing, meetings and action.

In other words, these parents have deployed core social democratic principles and practices to try and defend the interests of the local community against those of asset strippers from outside. It is precisely these kinds of commitment and engagement by the local community that may improve the lot of poor, disadvantaged children in the long term. If they had any common sense at all, politicians and bureaucrats would be trying to support the aspirations of the local community by fully funding and fully providing public schools in high poverty neighbourhoods, not shackling disenfranchised families and communities to the requirements of a secret bean-counter's contract.

Go Study for the Economy

Sandra Grey & Charles Sedgwick

For three decades, students and staff have faced continuing and fundamental changes in the tertiary education sector. Higher education has been transformed from a public good, funded collectively, to a private good which comes at a large personal cost. We have moved a long way from Fraser and Beeby's basic belief that every New Zealander had a "right as a citizen, to a free education" to the limits of their capability.[1] Tertiary education has become increasingly a 'private benefit' to satisfy a market, not citizens' preferences, capabilities or aspirations.

But the shift has not simply been one from state provision of tertiary education for the public good to free-market delivery at private cost. Like much of the public sector, the government is using 'market' mechanisms to regulate, control, and discipline the tertiary education 'industry' to satisfy its economic policy. Repeatedly the government says: "what is good for the economy is good for us all". Likewise, students are forced to act instrumentally, getting credentials which supposedly translate into jobs, if one believes the government.

For students (and their families), debt becomes an integral part of an entire lifetime. According to Joanna Wane in a *North and South* article on tertiary education, "Now, rather than a rite of passage, for many it's a time of extended dependence on their parents. It's an expensive way to tread water until 'real life' begins."[2] However, high levels of youth unemployment, low wages, and the casualisation of work, mean the 'real life' that students are entering is uncertain and unpredictable.

The changes to tertiary education have been founded on a free-market philosophy – a seemingly endless process that has altered the nature of how we as a nation view higher learning. Wendy Larner sees New Zealand's neoliberal project as going through three distinct phases, starting with the 1980s, when the state withdrew from many areas of economic production. It then went on to marketisation and more authoritarian policies around conditions for those not in work. Finally it moved to a 'partnering' phase, where discourses of 'social inclusion' and 'social investment' sat awkwardly alongside economic globalisation, free-market ideals, and contractualism.[3] With the changes in tertiary education, we follow Jamie Peck and Adam Tickell and argue that New Zealand has followed a path of 'roll-back' and 'roll-out' neoliberalism:

> … a shift from the pattern of deregulation and dismantlement so dominant during the 1980s, which might be characterised as 'roll-back neoliberalism', to an emergent phase of active state-building and regulatory reform – an ascendant moment of 'roll-out neoliberalism'.[4]

In the 1990s, the roll-back from providing public tertiary education meant that the state moved to create a competitive 'industry' driven by consumer demand. Tertiary education institutions competed in the new 'open market', with government funding attached to each student enrolled.

These roll-back reforms became a problem for governments and public-sector officials because, in part, the mass-market model created a strong increase in enrolments in higher education. In 1990, just over 20% of those aged 18–24 years were studying at tertiary education institutions. By 1998, this had risen to 32%.[5] Governments saw this development as unacceptable due to the rising costs to taxpayers which resulted from the larger numbers of New Zealanders in tertiary studies and the spread of courses and education providers to meet this rising 'consumer demand'.

The government presented the problem as inefficient use of funding by institutions.[6] Their solution was 'strategic steering' – more active control by government of the direction and management of tertiary education. From 2000, governments turned the mass-market, competitive model into a heavy-handed 'industry', regulated by government and focused squarely on economic growth and labour-market productivity. This led to policies such as capping student numbers; tighter targeting of funding; reducing duplication of programmes and institutions; and creating institutional 'strategic investment plans'. The philosophy pushing 'strategic steering' was the belief that the education system, left to itself, was incapable of recognising economic realities.[7]

Successive governments firmly linked policy[8] with goals, priorities and objectives tied to the nation's three-year election cycle. "Strong fiscal and performance imperatives require a further lift in tertiary education performance *over the next term of Government*" (emphasis added).[9] In particular, they recast the purpose of tertiary education and refocused it as a driver of economic growth and labour-market productivity.[10] They saw students as empty vessels to be filled with instrumental job skills.

This was the roll-out phase of neoliberalism – a phase where governments used policy processes and funding to control who gets to study, what they study, where and when. Gone are the broader goals of tertiary education such as creating actively engaged citizens and life-long learners. In their place, tertiary education has to produce good tax payers and workers. The National-led government 'targets' its investment to learners aged 18–25[11] through policies that "have the potential to provide better return on government expenditure in tertiary education".[12] Alongside age, government uses other criteria to ensure only the "right" students are admitted to tertiary study. It sees "little value for anyone if learners enrol in tertiary provision that they are unlikely to complete, or which lacks a clear progression to higher-level study".[13] This approach leads to 'risk aversion', which means that changes to the student loan and allowance policies can often exclude those studying part-time or those who have struggled with formal education.

The government focus on economic goals also shapes the type of courses offered and where they are taught.[14] Many courses at lower levels have been closed, often with little concern for the impact on learners and communities. The Ministry of Education wants to ensure it is "redirecting government expenditure away from low value spending, such as adult and community education courses for personal interest, towards higher value spending, such as degree level study."[15] 'Low-value' programmes of study have been cast adrift even though many have been crucial in advancing the position of not only individuals but their families and communities. For example, tertiary staff tell the story of how one member of the family enrolled in a Rural Education Activities Programme:

> … that led to three generations of the family participating in adult education. Four of the five family members have now graduated and developed a love of learning. The grandfather, three daughters, one son and one mokopuna, all participating in tertiary education through wānanga. This shows the importance of learning amongst familiar people in a familiar environment.[16]

The focus on economics and efficiency has led not only to savage cuts to community education and programmes around the country but also to the variety of subjects offered. The minister has moved to reduce courses with "poor long-term prospects" that don't lead to jobs.[17]

The Government's steering of the sector to achieve economic goals has markedly altered teaching and learning conditions. Academics are told to "work more efficiently", and that means less time spent on students and more on international-peer-reviewed research. Cost savings come through using more casual staff in teaching and increasing class sizes. In 2008 the student staff ratio was 17.9:1 and by 2010 it was 19.8:1. These 'economic efficiencies' ignore the implications for teaching and learning. For example, at one polytechnic 24 students were put into a workshop with only 16 welding bays.[18] This means less one-on-one tutorial help for the students and poses a major health and safety risk for staff and students. Such efficiency measures are happening at a time when the Tertiary Education Commission has underspent its funding for teaching and learning in the sector by $78m.[19]

There have been corresponding changes to the 'student body'. The government's focus on tertiary education as a private good has led to rising costs for individual students and their families. New Zealand is one of the nine OECD countries where the student's private payment exceeds 30% of the total income of tertiary educational institutions.[20] Yet there are no jobs at the end for many students and no evidence of an active labour market policy (all cost and risk is placed in private hands). So students take on heavy loans in a context of high youth unemployment (17.1% in 2013) and low wages. The Finance Minister has been quoted as saying that student-loan repayments were lower than expected, since graduates earned less than forecast.[21] As one parent noted in a *North and South* survey, "I feel there is no guarantee my child will gain employment in her field at the end of her studies. I have two other children who have begun degree studies which they decided were not taking them in the direction they wanted to go and ended up servicing significant loans as a result."[22] Student debt has long-term effects. As of March 2013, 714,942 'student borrowers' owed $13.5 billion (on average $18,883 each).[23]

Large numbers of students are poverty stricken,[24] overworked and often under-studied. The reality for most students is found in a university study guide:

> **Problem:** Despite using the Student Loan or getting an allowance, your total shortfall for weekly living costs plus all other expenses (emergencies, books, flat bonds, course related costs for example) could add up to more than $10,000 per year.[25]

All this adds up and students find themselves corralled into a narrowed hunt for credentials rather than knowledge. There seems to be little sense of belonging or commitment to community and nation. This should not be surprising given we have allowed their education to be re-cast not as a public good funded through public investment, but as a private good funded through significant private investment.

Tertiary Train-wreck – Unitec Design

David Cooke

Fifty academic staff in the Department of Design and Visual Arts at Unitec were dismissed in 2013 as part of a restructuring process. Unitec replaced them with industry providers in part-time and itinerant positions. Another 17 staff were turned into 'managers'-, charged with delivering up to $30,000 per year from industry.

Through the process Unitec lost highly experienced and qualified staff skilled in academic, teaching and professional settings – and a swathe of institutional knowledge. It also lost the investment it had made in higher qualifications and professional development for its staff, along with a significant sector of its research culture, its scholarship, its critical thinking – and its institutional integrity. As a result, it will lose reputation and standing as a leading school of design, greatly respected throughout the country. To compound the problem, it will lose potential employment for its graduates, who have consistently benefited from all these factors.

What it has gained is a massive burden for remaining staff. The new, depleted force is now expected to cater to over 500 students in different levels and years. Ominously, it will also gain an eager audience of other tertiaries keen to do the same sort of thing.

Why is this happening? It's because Unitec management has bought into the ideology of corporate colonising that has characterised New Zealand life since the 1980s. This business-first mantra is simply at odds with critical, enlightened education.

Unitec's ideology is also an embarrassing contradiction. For years it has insisted on its staff being able to span industry, academe and pedagogy. It energetically pushed staff to gain and upgrade formal academic and professional qualifications. It has called repeatedly for staff to perform well on research, for the institution to score well on rankings in the Performance-Based Research Fund.

Unitec has swept away a culture that took years to construct. It now relies on casual labour that is unprepared for tertiary teaching, thereby undermining and weakening the teaching profession.

Adapted from original article on Scoop, 2013

Students are relatively powerless to stop degradation of the sector, even though they contribute to the cost of education, because government steering is what controls behaviour of staff and management. There is certainly no room for 'student activism' in the government-controlled tertiary education industry, particularly following the move to voluntary student unionism, which further depoliticises an already dispirited student body. Students, now seen as stakeholders, are subject to 'satisfaction surveys',[26] yet often excluded from decision-making in the managerial tertiary education institution.

Over a generation, since the introduction of the mass-market, private-good approach to tertiary education, current students have little or no memory of anything other than fees, loans, and an uncertain future. Those who govern and administer tertiary education, despite their own experience of a free education system and all that it provided, offer little or no respite. These factors mean there are only small pockets of resistance in our tertiary education system. This is in contrast to nations such as the United Kingdom, Canada and Chile, where students have held massive public demonstrations and in some cases achieved substantial change.[27] This has even affected the fatalistic way students discuss their loans:

> It's just one of those things that unless you're lucky enough to have a massive trust fund and pay cash for your fees, it's just one of those things in life and you have to suck it up. If you want to better your life, pay the money.[28]

So there are clear problems in narrowing the way education is viewed to a focus on the economy and labour-market productivity. When tertiary education is defined purely as a form of (self-interested) private investment, we lose goals such as promoting a love of learning, fostering public debate, and enhancing democratic citizenship.[29] The mistake is that in disciplining tertiary education institutions to focus on "economic gain and labour market productivity", governments assume that it is possible to accurately predict and provide for the demands of the labour market – it is not. Moreover, a crucial range of social, political, and human benefits (such as creating a sense of community, being a responsible critic and conscience of society, being a 'good citizen', or being a repository of knowledge and culture for the good of all publics) that come from tertiary education (if recognised at all) are seen only as the icing on the cake, not the core purpose of education.

The lack of focus on the 'public good' and 'public outcomes' of education comes at a critical time in history when our world faces major social, economic and environmental problems. We desperately need the tertiary education sector to help develop critically engaged and innovative citizens to tackle these issues.

It is therefore time to reclaim an education system as a public good not a private right or limited entitlement for the rich. It must be equitably financed "and dedicated to educating all young people as compassionate, critical, thoughtful and knowledgeable citizens".[30]

1 Beeby, C.E. (1983). 'Centennial Address' NZEI, *National Education*, 65(3), pp. 106–110.

2 Wane, J. (2013). "The Paper Chase", *North and South*, Dec 2013, p. 42.

3 Larner, W. (2003). "Guest editorial: Neoliberalism?", *Environment and Planning D: Society and Space*, 21(5), p. 510.

4 Peck, J. and Tickell, A. (2002). "Neoliberalizing Space", *Antipode*, Vol 34 (3), p. 384.

5 Ministry of Education (1998). "Profile & Trends 1998: New Zealand's tertiary education sector", Education Counts, The New Zealand Ministry of Education, Wellington, p. 23. Retrieved from www.educationcounts.govt.nz/publications/series/2531/profile__and__trends_1998_new_zealands_tertiary_education_sector

6 Ministry of Education (2006). "OECD Thematic Review of Tertiary Education: New Zealand Country Background Report", The New Zealand Ministry of Education, Wellington, p. 135. January 2006. Retrieved from www.oecd.org/education/skills-beyond-school/36441052.pdf

7 Mahoney, P. (2003). "Tertiary Education Funding – Overview of Recent Reform", Parliamentary Library, Wellington, p. 4.

8 See Ministry of Education (2006), p. 4.

9 Ministry of Education (2011). Briefing to the Incoming Minister, Ministry of Education, Wellington, December 2011, p. 3.

10 McLaughlin, M. (2003). "Tertiary Education Policy in New Zealand", Research Report, Ian Axford (NZ) Fellowships in Public Policy; Zepke, N. (2012). "What of the Future for Academic Freedom in Higher Education in Aotearoa New Zealand?," Policy Futures in Education, 10(2); and, TEC (2008) Briefing to the Incoming Minister, Tertiary Education Commission, National Office, Wellington, November 2008.

11 New Zealand Treasury (2011). Briefing to the Incoming Minister of Finance: Increasing Economic Growth and Resilience, New Zealand Treasury, Wellington, p. 21.

12 Ministry of Education (2008). Briefing to the Incoming Minister, Ministry of Education, Wellington, November 2008, p. 11.

13 Ministry of Education (2011), p. 30.

14 For example, the "significant wage premium for people who complete higher-level study, particularly bachelor's degrees" outlined in the Tertiary Education Strategy 2010–2015, has impacted upon the courses institutions choose to teach.

15 Ministry of Education (2011), p. 11.

16 Grey, Sedgwick and Scott (2013), p. 14.

17 MacDonald (2013) says "Those degrees with poor long-term prospects are likely to be affected by [the Minister of Tertiary Education] Joyce's plans to make job success a performance indicator for tertiary education providers and to review their fee

subsidies to ensure they're not perversely promoting degrees with poor prospects." www.stuff.co.nz/dominion-post/news/9110729/Graduates-frustrated-at-lack-of-jobs/

18 Grey, S., Sedgwick, C. and Scott, J. (2013) "Te Kaupapa Wahioranga: The Blueprint for Tertiary Education", Tertiary Education Union, Wellington, November 2013, p. 19. Retrieved from teu.ac.nz/wp-content/uploads/2013/11/TKW.pdf

19 Houkamau, James (2013). Press release, Tertiary Education Union, 16 November 2013.

20 OECD (2006) Emergence of Private Higher Education Funding within the OECD Area, Kiira Kärkkäinen September 2006, www.oecd.org/dataoecd/19/20/38621229.pdf

21 Fox, M. (2013). "Generational pay gap evident in figures", *The Dominion Post* 9 October 2013, p. A2.

22 Wane (2013), p. 42.

23 Jones, Nicholas (2013). "Budget 2013: Tardy student borrowers owe $427m." *New Zealand Herald*, 18 May 2013.

24 Scoop Media (2012). "Study Shows 15% of Students in 'Absolute Financial Distress.'" Retrieved from www.scoop.co.nz/stories/ED1204/S00076/study-shows-15-of-students-in-absolutefinancial-distress.htm also see www.glsnz.org.nz

25 Victoria University of Wellington (2013). "Financial Survival: Make sure you control your money, so it doesn't control you". Retrieved from www.victoria.ac.nz/students/money/financial-survival

26 Institutions lure students with advertising totalling $30 million annually in New Zealand. See Elder, V. (2012). "University spends $2.2m on advertising", *Otago Daiy Times* Online News Retrieved from www.odt.co.nz/campus/university-otago/226992/university-spends-22madvertising

27 Gordon Campbell (2013). Chile Promises Free University Education to All, werewolf.co.nz/2013/12/chile-buries-the-pinochet-era-again/

28 Pearl, H. and Chris Hillock (2013). "Waikato's billion-dollar student debt loan burden". Retrieved from www.stuff.co.nz/waikato-times/news/8755868/Waikatos-billion-dollar-studentloan-burden

29 Roberts, Peter (1999). "The Future of the University: Reflections from New Zealand", *International Review of Education*, 45(1), p. 80.

30 Giroux, Henry (2013). "Hope in the Age of Looming Authoritarianism", *Truth Out*, 2 December 2013, p. 8. Retrieved from truth-out.org/opinion/item/20307-hope-in-the-age-of-looming-authoritarianism

Controlling Curriculum: Controlling People

Anne-Marie O'Neill

> Curriculum is the collective story we tell our children about our past, our present and future.[1]

Successive waves of free-market thinking have imposed a top-down management and accountability system on education and the school curriculum. Based on standards, assessments and measurement of performance outputs, this has changed the purpose of schooling, the nature of school knowledge and learning. It has reshaped teacher professionalism on the basis of mistrust for teachers' professional knowledge and judgement. By imposing content, assessment and teaching, it aims to make teachers obedient technicians – rather than independent, creative, thinking professionals, mindful and active around their ethical and political responsibilities. This system has moved the curriculum away from valuing and strengthening the collective 'public good' and the creation of well-rounded, thoughtful citizens. Instead, it aims to produce individualistic, competitive and commercially enterprising human capital who will 'add value' to themselves, the labour market and our economic competitiveness. This chapter sets out the basic assumptions and changes to curriculum and its assessment, over the last 25 years of neoliberal, market-driven change.

The big questions

In essence the curriculum is distilled from social, cultural, political and economic processes. Two features play a big part. One is hidden knowledge – e.g. realities of class, gender and culture. The other is excluded knowledge – content that's missing – in what is known as the "null" curriculum. Curricula also raise and answer basic questions about:

> *What* and *whose* knowledge we ought to impart to our young
>
> What *value* we ought to assign to teachers and what *role* they ought to have in educating; and

> What *kind* of society we ought to seek, what *kind* of relationships and social structures … human qualities, skills and personal relationships we ought to foster.[2]

At one level we see this in recent calls for the curriculum to 'fix' all manner of social ills by teaching students to: handle aggressive dogs; save for retirement; drive safely; develop water survival and rugby skills; reduce pregnancies; and counter a porn and rape culture. Under the surface of curriculum assumptions and in its daily practice, however, lie issues of power, control and *social justice.* Not only do curriculum and assessment shape societies and their populations in terms of the dominant social, cultural and economic ideas, they stream individuals into production, future resources and life chances.

A little history

In 1877, when 'universal, compulsory and secular' education began in Aotearoa, its aim was to produce literate, compliant and productive worker-voter-citizens and to preserve the social hierarchy. National Standards (NS) examinations publically evaluated pupils, schools and teachers. The state saw the curriculum and assessment as forms of educational and social control and monitored them very closely. This reflected the dominant views of the times. For example, girls were never banned from accessing secondary-school knowledge. It was simply assumed they would not. When they did, doctors campaigned to make their curriculum totally domestic. The state also tried to prevent Māori boys accessing the academic curriculum, and future professions and business, to keep them in farming and labour.

Upon election, the first Labour Government (1935–49) dropped examinations, broadened content and set up an activity-based, child-centred curriculum to develop well-rounded citizens. Assessment was mainly for learning rather than accountability. Educational standards reflected an 'ideal' of the teacher as an *improving* professional, making informed judgements in partnership with the state. During the 1970s–80s, however, the curriculum, teachers and their supportive profession came under steady attack. By the late 1980s, the Treasury and powerful business and corporate groups pushed to reform both the administration and the curriculum. For the latter this began with the election of the fourth National Government (1990–99).

1990s: Curriculum and assessment change

In 1991, in line with the state-sector reforms, National overlaid the curriculum and its assessment with a national standards, reporting and accountability framework. This *radically* changed the very nature, essence and purpose of schooling, teachers' work, the curriculum and its assessment. It reshaped the 'new' school curriculum as a management and reporting process away from its educational purposes. The curriculum is now oriented towards the 'new' economy: the needs of our affluent Asian trading partners; an expanding service sector; continual retraining; and the loss of manual jobs. Consequently, school curricula and increasingly that of the early childhood and tertiary sectors, have become:

- prescribed as outcomes
- predictable
- driven by external, non-educational purposes
- related to work
- monitored; and
- measured

This reflects their *remaking* as processes which:

- are economic, rather than educational
- allow the state to 'steer' education, individuals and society from the centre
- are vehicles of cultural change; and
- measure and evaluate national and international competitiveness.

Building an 'Enterprise Culture'

National's notorious 1991 budget undid universal welfare, deregulated the labour market and brought in extreme cost-cutting to build an 'Enterprise Culture'. As part of *competitive commercialisation*, welfare cuts took over a billion dollars from the poor during the 1990s. This was supposedly to throw out the culture of dependency and poor economic performance of the welfare state.

National reshaped what it saw as the curriculum's "excessive focus on social issues and poor preparation for the competitive world". Its purpose became economic and the curriculum and assessment were fully integrated into economic policy. According to the Minister of Education, "a new culture of enterprise and competition in the curriculum .... lay at the core of personal and national economic transformation".[3]

Under the welfare state, people were understood to have basic needs and citizenship rights to shelter, education, health and welfare. In free-market states like ours, the market replaces the concept of society, inequality keeps people ready and willing to work and drives down the cost of labour and the main rights that are prioritised are property ownership and law and order. Individuals are responsible for their 'own' outcomes. As human capital, people are counted as costs, productive units, investments and outputs. Importantly, the qualities of humans can be *reshaped* and *remade* as the economy and markets demand.

Modelled on Thatcher's Britain, the National Government's 'Enterprise Culture' encouraged people to remake themselves as enterprises, following business practices. The official line emphasised aggressive individualism, commercialisation and risk-taking, in order to improve productivity and global competitiveness. It downplayed collective responsibility and social action. Individuals were to become economic entrepreneurs, producer/consumers and 'autonomous choosers' in marketplaces. Unbeknown to most people, this transformation was to occur primarily through education, particularly the school curriculum and its assessment.

1993: The New Zealand Curriculum Framework

In the 1960s, the education profession began pushing for learning goals, knowledge and assessment, based on stated principles or criteria in order to make learning clearer and fairer for all rather than the elite who could cope with examinations. However, outcomes-based curricula had emerged in the United States from the 1950s as a technical model of control for producing particular kinds of people. This was based on Frederick Taylor's 'scientific management' model of the economic 'efficiency' of humans, machines and factory production from the 1900s. When applied to curriculum, supporters claimed two benefits from stating curriculum outcomes: you could 'scientifically' predict learner behaviour and you could measure it 'objectively' – just like machines.

The 1993 New Zealand Curriculum Framework[4] was modelled on the latter assumptions. It copied the reforming OECD economies, such as the UK, the USA, Canada and Australia – prescribed by a central ministry and driven by assessment, it sought to prescribe, measure outputs and control knowledge and learning.

The OECD is now a major influence on our national policy-making, advocating market-based policies, a standardised, hierarchical and competitive curricula for its member nations. Along with the influence of international educational testing, it has ensured our curriculum is international rather than national.

In the current model, the state lays out 'standards' and social goals, then sets out to measure them. These mechanisms of control assume teachers will be more effective if told *what* to teach and *what* and *how* to assess. The Curriculum is broken down into hundreds of curriculum goals called Achievement Objectives (AOs). This curriculum structure has no foundations in educational research, practice or theory.[5] The main purpose of structures based on outcomes is that they appear to be scientific and they enable the central selection (and control) of certain kinds of knowledge and supposedly, 'objective' measurement of students.

During the 1990s, teachers tested hundreds of poorly designed AOs, trying them out as national standards. The reason was that the Education Review Office wanted reliable data to measure 'worth' for performance pay – and to create a competitive market between schools. In an 'assessment frenzy', testing of students increased, with accountability becoming more important than learning by the late 1990s.[6] Primary teachers had to install a measurement regime and culture,[7] just like their secondary colleagues. National attempted unsuccessfully to introduce national testing in 1998, on the basis that teachers' judgements could not be trusted. This would have further 'disciplined' teachers and students and strengthened competitive measurement.

In its Essential Skills, the Curriculum favoured vocational skills, English, mathematics, science and technology with a commercial focus and increased assessment. Central features of primary and secondary curricula are enterprise education and profit-making initiatives. While the primary curriculum has narrowed dramatically, the secondary curriculum has widened to also offer more commercial, vocational options, such as business studies.

By the end of the 1990s, the policy focus moved on to helping 'at risk' groups and to lifting community 'effectiveness' to strengthen family involvement in learning. The failure of national testing led to a Literacy and Numeracy Strategy and standardised assessment. The Labour Government's (1999–2008) desire for a 'knowledge economy' demanded a culture of continuous improvement and review, plus achievement data as evidence of teacher effectiveness and learning.

2007: The New Zealand Curriculum

A highly orchestrated review resulted in a revised Curriculum in 2007.[8] It reduced AO numbers, encouraged school-based curricula and replaced "essential skills" with "competencies." These came from an OECD project requiring teachers to support features like self-discipline. Extending the enterprise project, competencies are expected to create a 'well-functioning' society, increase productivity and decrease welfare costs.

Like National, the Labour Government built a vast monitoring, disciplining and controlling process around curriculum and assessment during the 2000s. Teachers had to undertake continuous 'upskilling' to lift their effectiveness, 'quality' and outcomes. Ministry provided exemplars for each subject, set out specific content and teaching practices, *including* teacher questions and responses to students. Exemplars leave little for teachers to have to think about if teachers choose to use them in this way. Standardised assessments and pre-prepared materials have become increasingly important. By taking on 'upskilling', teachers accepted both responsibility for educational 'underachievement' *and* for raising it. They also gave away control of their own professional oversight in favour of mandatory state procedures.

2008: The National Coalition Government

The standards-based curriculum framework enabled the National Coalition Government (2008–) to revive its national testing agenda. A year after its election, in 2009, it introduced National Standards (NS) in reading, writing and mathematics. These are broad descriptions and models of what students in Years 1–8 "must know and be able to do at the end of each period or year of schooling" (Ministry of Education, 2009, p. 6). Competency[9] is assessed twice a year by teachers using Overall Teacher Judgements (OTJs), using standardised assessments and observation. Serious professional concerns around NS include a lack of trials, variation in interpreting the standards and validity issues. There are also serious dangers in interpreting school 'worth' or 'quality' from crude school league tables. School outcomes primarily reflect the socio-economic catchment area of the school and the backgrounds of the students. Such standards seriously narrow our school curriculum, the professional practice and judgement of teachers and, most importantly, label children (and teachers and schools) failures or successes.

At the end of 2012, National released unreliable NS data on 1,899 schools. This came after the Ministry published its own research revealing a large range in accuracy in the Overall Teacher Judgements. The 2013 data was also dismissed by educationalists as unsuitable for drawing meaningful conclusions.

From 2015, the Ministry will insist on schools using a Progress and Consistency Tool (PaCT),[10] educational software to "assist teacher judgements" in the assessment of the NS.

With the streamlining of assessment methodologies, NS will function as a national test.

The National Government's educational policies seek to radically extend the market agenda through privatisation and competition, including: support for private schools, Public–Private Partnerships, highly paid Charter Schools, attempts to extend class sizes, National Standards/testing, performance pay and its 'out of the blue' January 2014 announcement of Investing in Educational Success (IES). Like NS, IES is based on a weak evidence base and no consultation with the sector. $359 million will be spent on imposing yet another business model on education.

This will set up communities of schools based on lead schools, collaboration and new roles for teachers. In primary schools, National Standards data will likely identify 'executive' and 'change' principals and 'lead' and 'expert' teachers, incentivised by salary increases, to tackle and rectify underachievement. The communities will set Achievement Objectives and targets and shifts in NS data or designated outcomes will be evidence of success. New professional standards are to be devised. Once in place, the apparatus will be established for the introduction of: performance pay, non-educational managers, private 'service' providers, centrally stipulated ways of practising and managing and, importantly, bulk funding.

This policy will entrench NS further into schools. It will also entrench and strengthen the measurement regime and culture established in schools and it could further strengthen a competitive market and school 'choice'. It will not reduce the long tail of underachievement because educational inequalities have their primary cause in societal inequalities. Aotearoa is one of the most unequal societies in the developed world and the current government has pursued policies that have secured this (e.g. tax cuts for the wealthy).

Conclusion

There is plenty to respond to. We need to challenge the view of:

- our young as economic capital, products or instruments for the service of ever-changing markets and international competitiveness;
- teachers as deficient in knowledge and skills, as obedient technical functionaries and risk managers on behalf of the state; and
- 'education as economics'.

The anti-educational, unethical, non-research based and politically driven assumptions and practices of the National-Māori-Act Coalition Government distort the "collective story we tell our children", through the curriculum. But they also change the fundamental and deep-seated meanings of what it is to be human, to be an educated and thinking person, the nature and role of knowledge and the curriculum, the nature of teaching and learning and the nature and definition of success.

The primary teachers' union, the New Zealand Educational Institute (NZEI), has demonstrated exemplary sector leadership over National's term in office. As parents and an *informed* public, we can support their sustained critiques and demand an *educational* research base and *democratic,* inclusive policy processes of our politicians and state agencies. We can support this by asking questions of politicians in the media and demanding media investigations of the full complexity of educational issues. We further need to question and state the limitations of narrow, questionable and unethical forms of measurement that service economic conceptions and markets, as an indicator of educational achievement and success. We also need to seriously challenge education as an economic process and indicator and affirm its role as a 'public good' rather than a private 'product'. Mostly, we need to reaffirm the human dignity of our students and teachers, which economic/instrumental conceptions and processes of education do not.

1 Grumet, M. R. (1981, 115). Restitution and reconstruction of educational expereince: an autobiographical method for curriculum theory. In Lawn, M. & Barton, L. (Eds). *Rethinking curriculum Studies: A radical approach* (115–130) Croom Helm: London.

2 O'Neill, A-M. Clark, J. and Openshaw, R. (2004, 18). Introduction. In A-M. O'Neill, J. Clark, & R. Openshaw (Eds), *Reshaping knowledge culture and learning: Policy and content in the New Zealand Curriculum Framework* (pp. 143–160). Palmerston North: Dunmore Press.

3 Smith, L. (1991, 1–8). *Education policy: Investing in people our greatest asset.* Wellington: Government Print.

4 Ministry of Education (1993). *The New Zealand curriculum framework* . Wellington: Learning Media.

5 Elley, W. (2004, 91–108). Curriculum reform in retrospect: Was it forward or backward? In A-M. O'Neill, J. Clark, & R. Openshaw (Eds), *Reshaping knowledge culture and learning: Policy and content in the New Zealand Curriculum Framework* (pp. 91–108). Palmerston North: Dunmore Press.

6 Hill, M. (1999, 180–184). Assessment in self-managing schols: Primary teachers balancing learning and accountability demands in the 1990s. *New Zealand Journal of Educational Studies, 34* (1), 176–185.

7 Biesta, G. J. J. (2010). *Good education in an age of measurement: Ethics, politics, democracy.* Boulder, Colorado: Paradigm publishers.

8 Ministry of Education. (2007). *The New Zealand Curriculum.* Wellington: Learning Media.

9 Ministry of Education. (2009, 6). *Mathematics standards for years 1–8.* Wellington: Ministry of Education.

10 Ministry of Education. (2011). *Progress and consistency tool.* http://assessment.tki.org.nz/News/Progress-and-Consistency-tool (Accesssed March 4 2012).

References

Biesta, G. J. J. (2010). *Good education in an age of measurement: Ethics, politics, democracy.* Boulder, Colorado: Paradigm publishers.

Elley, W. (2004). Curriculum reform in retrospect: Was it forward or backward? In A-M. O'Neill, J. Clark, & R. Openshaw (Eds), *Reshaping knowledge culture and learning: Policy and content in the New Zealand Curriculum Framework* (pp. 91–108). Palmerston North: Dunmore Press.

Experts Advisory Group on Solutions to Child Poverty (2012). *Solutions to child poverty in New Zealand: Evidence for action.* Auckland: Office of the Children's Commissioner.

Grumet, M. R. (1981). Restitution and reconstruction of educational expereince: an autobiographical method for curriculum theory. In Lawn, M. & Barton, L. (Eds). *Rethinking curriculum studies: A radical approach* (115–130) Croom Helm: London.

Grundy, S. (1987). *Curriculum: product or praxis.* London: Falmer Press.

Hall, C. (2005). The National Cetrtificate of Educational Achievement (NCEA) *Is there a Third Way?* In J. Codd, & K. Sullivan (Eds), *Education policy directions in Aotearoa New Zealand* (pp. 235–265). Victoria: Thomson Dunmore Press.

Hill, M. 1999. Assessment in self-managing schols: Primary teachers balancing learning and accountability demands in the 1990s. *New Zealand Journal of Educational Studies, 34* (1), 176–185.

Ministry of Education. (1993). *The New Zealand curriculum framework .* Wellington: Learning Media.

Ministry of Education. (2007). *The New Zealand curriculum.* Wellington: Learning Media.

Ministry of Education. (2009). *Mathematics standards for years 1–8.* Wellington: Ministry of Education.

Ministry of Education. (2011). *Progress and consistency tool.* assessment.tki.org.nz/News/Progress-and-Consistency-tool (Accesssed March 4 2012).

Ministry of Education. (2012). *National standards: School sample monitoring & evaluation project 2011.* www.educationcounts.govt.nz (Accessed October 6 2012).

Neyland, J. (2004) An ethical critique of the paradigm case: the mathematics curriculum. In A-M. O'Neill, J. Clark, & R. Openshaw (Eds), *Reshaping knowledge culture and learning: Policy and content in the New Zealand Curriculum Framework* (pp. 143–160). Palmerston North: Dunmore Press.

Smith, L. 1991. *Education policy: Investing in people our greatest asset.* Wellington: Government Print.

More Markets, Less Democracy

Sandra Grey

The last decade has been marked by strong demands for greater democracy in many parts of the world: witness the Arab Spring and the Occupy movement. In New Zealand too, citizens have made repeated demands for a greater connection between the government and the people, such as the open letter sent to Prime Minister John Key by The Rally for Democracy, Canterbury, in December 2012; the Rally for Democracy held in Nelson in August 2013; and web-based campaigns such as Public Good, Kiwis connect, and Rebuild the future Christchurch. We are seeing a surge in demands for popular sovereignty – that ordinary people should be involved in creating the rules that affect their world and their lives.

On all international measures, New Zealand is a democratic nation. We have free and fair elections, low levels of corruption – according to Transparency International – and our fundamental rights are protected by the Bill of Rights Act 1990. So why has the New Zealand public been questioning whether the actions of our political elite – our government – are democratic? The calls for greater democratic engagement in the last three decades show that people are deeply frustrated with our liberal representative democracy. They are frustrated with the actions of successive governments that stick to free-market principles in running the country – hollowing out the way our democracy works.

While much has been written about how free-market principles have changed the nature of New Zealand's state, society and economy, there is little analysis on the way they affect democracy itself. It is timely to ask whether market-focused governments protect the core democratic principles of popular control (the ideal that the people should have some control over decisions that affect their world and their lives) and human equality.[1]

Both scholars and citizens should be concerned that successive market-focused governments in New Zealand have constrained and even eroded these core democratic principles. Market-focused governments have undermined popular sovereignty by claiming that "there is no alternative" (TINA) to a free-market approach to state and society; by creating a political climate which rules out of order collective action by citizens; and by pushing a policy agenda which leads to rising inequalities in society – inequalities that affect political and civil rights.

Hollowing out democracy

New Zealand governments since 1984 have argued that the only way to distribute goods and services in our society is through an open and 'free' market. In doing so, they have taken the politics out of politics.[2] The last Labour-led government represented itself as pragmatic, grounded, and less ideological[3] than previous governments. This approach has continued under the National-led government since 2008. Economic policies that are used to drive social reform have important political implications, but they are represented as neutral questions of technical expertise.[4] And governments following this approach quickly dismiss any citizens who criticise the political direction being imposed on the country. For example, when Grey Power and other groups presented a petition for a citizen-initiated referendum on asset sales to parliament in 2013, the Finance Minister stated it would make no difference to the process.[5]

Governments dismiss the 'will of the people' by claiming they were given a 'mandate' at election-time. This immediately constructs a very restricted notion of democracy in which the 'will of the people' can only be executed and expressed at national elections.[6] It seems our democracy is now only a mechanism for creating governments and making sure that government power continues.[7]

Delegitimising collective action

The market-approach to politics and government has given political leaders a logic for ignoring 'the will of the people'. The idea is that all citizens who make claims on the government are acting out of self-interest, just as they would in economic markets. This public-choice logic means politicians can marginalise or put down almost any challenge to their actions – whether the criticisms come from long-standing citizen groups, unions, professional bodies such as teachers, or individuals. For example, in 2004, Prime Minister Helen Clark called citizens who took part in the major hikoi over the foreshore and seabed legislation "haters and wreckers". Additionally, in 2008, the Minister of Social Welfare publicly attacked two women who criticised the government's canning of the training incentive allowance.[8] And on Waitangi Day 2014, John Key condemned protestors, saying: "Most people go to Waitangi to have a great time but there are one or two people that go to cause trouble and use the media to advance their own causes and their own issues."[9] Whatever you think of the political issues behind protests, when politicians publicly dismiss the voice of citizens, they cut across the core democratic principle of popular control – our right as citizens to have a say in the rules that affect us. These actions create a climate of fear around speaking out on important public issues.[10]

The complete disregard for citizen lobbies is frustrating for community organisations that work with the most marginalised New Zealanders, leading groups to seek legal remedies and even take international action against the New Zealand government. For example, in 2013 the Law Society took a complaint to the UN over the poor level of consultation around the Public Health and Disability Amendment Bill.[11]

The market-focus of our government also helps to hollow out democracy by changing the relationship between state and society. In this market approach to government, contracting is the dominant mode of funding community social services and this creates a fear of 'biting the hand that feeds'. Over half of the respondents in a 2013 survey of NGOs noted that government contract funding would be cut for groups who spoke out.[12]

At the same time as creating a climate of fear created for citizen groups, successive governments have claimed to be efficient, technical managers of state, and this opens the way for strong cabinet control over political decision-making. Cabinet rule has long been a problem in New Zealand.[13] The current market-focused cabinet seems to be willingly and blatantly ignoring evidence from formal democratic processes such as the select committees and major government-led reviews that involve citizens and experts in issues like the 2013 MMP review. Even when thousands of citizens take part in a parliamentary select committee, as happened in discussions of changes to labour laws in 2013, the cabinet does not heed 'the will of the people'. Community and voluntary sector groups when surveyed in 2013 noted this approach. One noted [Under National] "There always seems to be a subtext of 'already made our minds up but we will listen' to appear like 'the good guys.'" And yet another stated that [Under National] there was a "… silencing of any discussion where different opinions other than the Minister's are attempting to be voiced."[14]

Cabinet control in political decision-making is cutting across local-level democracy and the role of public service officials and judiciary. The National-led government pushed through the Auckland super city against the wishes of many local communities. It trampled on local democratic institutions in

Canterbury following the 2011 earthquake.[15] Under the market-oriented governments, we have seen a shift in the interaction between the Cabinet Ministers and their own officials. This shift is seen in the interactions with the judiciary. For example in 2004, after criticism was raised about the Supreme Court's name and budget by the Chief Justice, Prime Minister Helen Clark said it was a good principle for judges to "stick to the bench".[16] Research by Kumarasingham and Power notes that the Attorney General has, for the first time, failed to defend the autonomy of the judiciary to speak out on matters of public importance. In fact he has joined other ministers in criticising the judiciary for their critiques of government actions.[17] This has prompted commentary by the judiciary and Chief Justice Dame Sian Elias has noted that in New Zealand "the independence of the judiciary from other sources of state power is fragile."[18]

The lack of time for consultation with government makes it harder for citizens to take part in democratic processes. Consultation periods on major policy and law changes are often as short as six weeks and governments continue to use urgency to rush through law changes.[19] In 2005, about 30 per cent of Parliament's sittings were taken outside its normal hours under 'urgency', moved by government ministers.[20] It seems the more-market governments have taken to heart the cautionary words of Labour Finance Minister Roger Douglas[21] – that the government should move quickly so that citizens had no time to mobilise against the major structural changes begun in 1984.

Rising inequalities hurt democracy

Added to these breaches of the core democratic principle of popular control over decision-making, the other basis of democracy – human equality – has been undermined by the more-market approach to state and society. We see rising economic inequality in New Zealand, often justified by a narrative about freedom of choice. But when 'the people' are constructed as consumer-citizens, freedom depends on access to resources. We have autonomy so long as we have the money to exercise that freedom (for example, the money for private medical care when the public health system falters). We have freedom to choose as long as we are flexible to market demands (for example, we are free to take work if we are prepared to move our family to another town to take a job).

But this market-approach to government does not provide citizens with the freedom to collectively ask questions and seek answers. Nor does it enable people to collectively look for a change in the direction of our government. The market approach denies that social rights (access to goods, services, and income) are crucial for ensuring full freedom in society.

Inequality between individuals is not the only factor that distorts our democracy. While market-oriented governments undermine collectives seeking to redistribute goods in society, there has been a consistent process favouring business in decision-making processes.[22] The rise of more-market approaches to government has led to a strong increase in the power of business lobbyists – a fact not missed by New Zealanders: 44% of those participating in a 2004 values survey stated that the nation was run by a few big interests looking out for themselves.[23]

Reclaiming our place in democracy

On both counts – popular control and equality – market-focused governments have failed to be governments "of the people, by the people, and for the people."[24] Successive governments have hollowed out our rights to speech, assembly, agitation, and the control we should have over the rules that govern us. And they have created a political climate in which fear and disillusionment limits dissent. Yet they express surprise at the world they have helped create. The Minister of Finance, Bill English, said in a 2010 speech, that the government was not being challenged enough: "We are not getting enough people kicking the door down saying you can do this really differently and here's how I am going to contribute, and here's how you can contribute."[25] The people have been trying to kick down the door for three decades but have been pushed back by governments who claim the only way forward is for them to efficiently manage our state, society, and economy using free-market principles.

In contrast, I would argue the only way forward is for citizens to reclaim a strong civil society – spaces free from institutional control – and for our politicians to recognise the importance of citizen-voices in running the country. We need to push back against "managed" electoral democracy where decisions are made for the people as opposed to arrived at by the people.[26] If we do not create a democratic system where politicians respect civil society agitation, the coming generations are likely to have two options: one is to accept all rules passed by the elected political elite, no matter how heinous or problematic; the other is to mount militant and costly protest actions. I think it is better for our society, economy, and future generations if we make sure our democracy is in good working order today.

1 See Henderson, J. and Bellamy, P. (2002). *Democracy in New Zealand: International IDEA Country Study*, Christchurch: Macmillan Brown Centre for Pacific Studies and International Institute for Democracy and Electoral Assistance; Democratic Audit UK, (2014). *Democratic Audit*, 2014. Retrieved from www.democraticaudit.com/

2 Bale, T. (2003). "Pricking the south sea bubble: From fantasy to reality in Labour-led New Zealand", *The Political Quarterly*, 74(2), p. 206.

3 Eichbaum, C. and Shaw, R. (2006) "Labour in government, social democracy, and the third way: the New Zealand experience," Paper for the British Political Studies Association Annual Conference, Reading University, 3–6 April, 2006.

4 Vázquez Arroyo, A. Y. (2008). "Liberal democracy and neoliberalism: A critical juxtaposition," *New Political Science*, 30(2), p. 155.

5 Rutherford, H. (2013, March 12). "Government to ignore asset sales referendum," Fairfax News. Retrieved from www.stuff.co.nz/national/politics/8412749/Government-to-ignore-asset-sales-referendum

6 Kumarasingham H. and Power, J. (2013). "Constrained parliamentarianism in the New Zealand regime," *Commonwealth and Comparative Politics*, 51(2), p. 238.

7 Heywood, A. (1992). *Political ideologies: An introduction*, Houndsmill, Baginstoke, Hampshire and London: Macmillan Education.

8 NZPA, (2009, 28 July). "Paula Bennett accused of Muldoon-style bullying," NZPA. Retrieved from www.stuff.co.nz/national/politics/2681539

9 Theunissen, M. and Ihaka, J. (2014, Feburary 4). "Waitangi celebrations start with scuffle," New Zealand Herald. Retrieved from www.nzherald.co.nz/nz/news/article.cfm?c_id=1&objectid=11196624

10 Grey S. and Sedgwick, C. (2013). "Fears, constraints and contracts: The democratic reality for New Zealand's community and voluntary sector," a report presented at the Community and Voluntary Sector Research Forum, Victoria University of Wellington, 26 March 2013.

11 Radio New Zealand, (2013, May 30). "Backlash grows over disabled carers bill," Checkpoint. Retrieved from www.radionz.co.nz/news/national/136458/backlash-grows-over-disabled-carers-bill

12 Commerer, J. Grey, S. and Sedgwick, C. (2014)."Fears, constraints and contracts," a presentation for the CADNZ Wellington, 11 February 2014, Wellington.

13 Palmer, G. and Palmer, M. (1997). *Bridled power: New Zealand government under MMP*, Auckland NZ/Oxford UK: Oxford University Press.

14 Commerer, J. Grey, S. and Sedgwick, C. (2014).

15 New Zealand Law Society (2010). "Law Society comments on Canterbury Earthquake Act," Press Release, 29 September 2010; B. Hayward, (2013). "The democracy-free zone," Blog, Public Address, 21 September 2012. Retrieved 4 February 2014 from publicaddress.net/speaker/the-democracy-free-zone

16 (2004). "Minister fires new shot at judges", *The New Zealand Herald*, 18 November 2004, www.nzherald.co.nz/nz/news/article.cfm?c_id=1&objectid=3611472

17 Kumarasingham, H. and Power, J. (2013).

18 In Kumarasingham, H. and Power, J. (2013). pp. 242–3.

19 See Ganley, M. (2000), "Select Committees and their role in keeping parliament relevant: Do New Zealand select committees make a difference?" Australasian

Study of Parliament Group (ASPG) Conference, *Parliament 2000: Towards a Modern Committee System 2001*, Brisbane, 2000.

20 Wood, A. G. (2005). "Globalization and parliament". In R. Patman and C. Rudd (Eds), *Sovereignty under seige? Globalization and New Zealand*, Aldershot: Ashgate.

21 Douglas, R. (1989). *Unfinished business*, Auckland NZ: Random House New Zealand.

22 Roper, B. (2006). "Business political activity in New Zealand from 1990 to 2005," *Kotuitui: New Zealand Journal of Social Sciences Online*, 1, pp. 161–183; Goldfinch, S. (2000). *Remaking New Zealand and Australian Economic Policy: Ideas, Institutions and Policy Communities*, Victoria University of Wellington.

23 Rose, E., Huakau, J., Huckel, T., Casswell, S., Perry, P., Howden-Chapman, P. and Duignan, P. (2005). "Public life values: A report from the New Zealand Values Study 2005," Centre for Social and Health Outcomes Research and Evaluation and Te Ropu Whariki, Massey University, Palmerston North, December 2005, p. 17.

24 Heywood, A. (1992), p. 272.

25 English, B. (2010). Speech to the Families Commission, Wellington.

26 Vázquez Arroyo, A. Y. (2008), p. 156.

Through the Smoke and Mirrors of Partnership

Michael A. Peters

The word 'partnership' generally refers to an undertaking between equals. In a free-market society, however, the terms of such agreements often mask an inherent inequality between the partners. I focus here on three types of partnership: the first involves the 'community'; the second is 'public–private partnerships'; the third uses digital social media to access and produce information and services known as the 'commons'.

The essential issue in partnerships concerns the power relations between the parties, especially when the relationship is between the state and the people, or a constituency or an institution. This raises the question of whether a genuine partnership is possible between such unequal entities, or whether the notion of partnership serves as a means of co-opting the less powerful participant.

1 Co-opting the community

'Partnership' in free-market economics is intended to draw together the state, the market, and civil society for entrepreneurial goals. The idea is to shift responsibility from the state onto communities. Official rhetoric about partnership is part of government practice for tying grassroots social democratic community action into a management strategy that involves the latter partner being governed from above. This kind of control by-passes community partnership and democratic action in favour of performance management techniques often dressed up as 'empowerment' and 'engagement'.

The education reforms introduced by the Lange Labour Government in 1989, known as 'Tomorrow's Schools', are an example where communities were co-opted to run schools according to principles set by the Ministry of Education.

2 Partnership as PPP: Gathering all before it

So-called public–private partnership (PPP) describes a government service that is funded through the private sector. The 'reform' of the public service sector has become a new and massive business opportunity worth billions of dollars. PPP is seen as a third-phase privatisation strategy, after state assets sales and mixed state enterprises, designed to privatise school property, hospitals, prisons, transport infrastructure and other remaining public assets. In free-market economics, it is seen as a low risk and low public perception strategy for the next phase of privatisation.

PPP is used as a tool of governing that clouds questions concerning ownership, authority and accountability. For instance, in a period in which the New Zealand government was looking for new school property, the Ministry of Education website refers to PPP in the following terms:

> A private partner is responsible for designing, building, financing and maintaining the school property for the term of the contract (usually 25 years from the opening of the school). The private partner works with the Ministry and the Establishment Board of Trustees (EBOT) to ensure the education vision for the school is captured in the design of the building.
>
> The Ministry of Education pays the private partner quarterly, with this payment reduced if the school facilities do not meet the standards specified in the contract. This effectively provides a 25-year guarantee on the buildings, unlike schools procured under traditional procurement models. The Government retains ownership of the land and buildings throughout the life of the contract.[1]

In March of 2014, Cabinet agreed that four new schools in Auckland, greater Christchurch and Queenstown would be delivered using a PPP.[2] It looks very likely that social infrastructure in New Zealand will be increasingly provided through these 'partnerships' at both national and local levels.[3] The website below details a conference on PPPs in New Zealand with the private-sector sponsors.

> PPPs have been embraced by overseas countries as a way of providing essential public services in a way that provides the most value for money. This model has only recently begun to gain some momentum here, with the construction of the first PPP schools and prisons underway and to be completed in the near future.[4]

PPPs are definitely on the agenda in a wide variety of projects, including education (school property), transport infrastructure, ultrafast broadband, prisons, primary health care (Investment in Human Capital Infrastructure").[5] As the *National Business Review*[6] (November 29, 2012) reported:

> Last week's government decision to go ahead with a PPP for the $1.3 billion Transmission Gully motorway north of Wellington should just be the beginning, Council for Infrastructure Development CEO Stephen Selwood says. "The PPP model is applicable right across the infrastructure sector, from roads to water supply, local councils, schools and hospitals. There are few sectors where the model does not have the potential to add value."

It is worth noting that the New Zealand Treasury's own analysis is not quite so rosy. It mentions problems and complex difficulties with tendering and negotiation, enforcing performance and political acceptability.[7]

3 An alternative vision: Partnership as the co-production of the commons as a public good

In their manifesto for co-production, the New Economics Foundation suggested that the traditional economic approach to public service is failing because "Neither markets nor centralised bureaucracies are effective models for delivering public services based on relationships." The Foundation defined co-production as the delivery of public services in an equal and reciprocal relationship between professionals, people using services, their families and their neighbours. It is based on a theory of the commons.

Commons are resources jointly shared by a group of people. The notion has experienced a huge revival since the mid-1980s. The internet today offers untapped possibilities for human creativity, global communication, and access to information to enable political discussion, free speech, and creativity needed for a healthy democracy.

In recent years, the emphasis has been on open democratic information resources and platforms that provide software and licensing commons. Resources like these promote open access in scientific communication, digital data-banks, institutional commons such as online libraries, as well as commons that are specific to certain subjects or disciplines.

The notion of the public sphere lies at the heart of the liberal theory of civil society. It features openness in communication and the production of public goods. The new public space of electronic and social media, unlike traditional industrial one-way broadcast media, is open and interactive. It carries many voices and lacks a central control or authority.

In liberal political economy the very distinction between public and private spheres is founded upon a concept of private property in an economy of scarcity. But with the new production of knowledge and a shift to the knowledge economy, open source and open access are encouraging new forms of collaboration that no longer hold that economic value is founded upon exclusive ownership. These new social forms, which depend upon new collectives based on networking, have the potential to transform the public sphere.

Free-market economics has undermined the nature of public knowledge and education institutions, through privatising education and monopolising knowledge flows. But education and science have always been wedded to principles of free inquiry and to the academic freedoms that are necessary to sustain the open society and social democracy.

These new platforms of open communication will restore the public nature of science and education and promote universal access to knowledge through economical ways of working together, including file-sharing, open archiving and open publishing.

Partnership in this new environment takes on a very different set of meanings.

1 www.minedu.govt.nz/NZEducation/EducationPolicies/Schools/PropertyToolBox/StateSchools/Funding/SchoolPropertyPPP.aspx

2 The relevant Cabinet paper is available at www.minedu.govt.nz/~/media/MinEdu/Files/EducationSectors/PrimarySecondary/PropertyToolbox/NewsAndEvents/PPP/PPPSchools-Project2CabinetPaper.pdf. On What is PPP? see www.minedu.govt.nz/~/media/MinEdu/Files/EducationSectors/PrimarySecondary/PropertyToolbox/NewsAndEvents/PPP/WhatisaPPPFactSheet.pdf

3 See the NZSIF discussion on PPP and the market potential for them at www.nzsif.co.nz/Social-Infrastructure/What-are-Public-Private-Partnerships/. See also www.infrastructure.govt.nz/publications/draftpppstandardcontract.

4 www.conferenz.co.nz/conferences/public-private-partnerships-new-zealand

5 See the sets of slides from the August 2013 conference at www.iscr.org.nz/f884,23447/ISCR_PPP_Conference_29_Aug_Presenters_PPTS_.pdf

6 See www.nbr.co.nz/article/ppps-key-nzs-future-infrastructure-checked-ca-133118

7 See www.treasury.govt.nz/publications/research-policy/ppp/2006/06-02/06.htm. See also the position paper of the Auckland Council at www.aucklandcouncil.govt.nz/SiteCollectionDocuments/aboutcouncil/mayorelectedrepresentatives/mayoralpositionpaperonppps20131127.pdf

A Just Society

David Cooke

Rebuilding

Twice in the 20th century, New Zealand came to international attention for its social reforms. The first was in the 1930s, when a Labour Government brought in the welfare state. As political analyst Bruce Jesson has noted, the initiative was not a thorough-going socialist alternative. But it was a dramatic push for social justice. There were many dimensions to it, but as one mother put it, "When we women received the Family Benefit, for the first time in our lives we had money of our own to spend on the children."

In the second milestone, in the 1980s, a Labour Government systematically cut back its own welfare state, in a process that was enthusiastically continued by successive National governments.

One remarkable difference between these two governments is that for once, in the 1930s, one of them actually acted in the better interests of the people it represented. It would be challenging to claim the same for the governments of John Key, Tony Abbott, David Cameron or Steven Harper.

Faced with the continuing damage from free-market forces in New Zealand, here's a simple three-step process for re-shaping society. First is to label and resist the kinds of sweeping changes that New Zealand governments made in the '80s and '90s. We are fully entitled to constantly monitor, analyse and contest the practice of free-market ideology. But some sectors of society have more room to move than others. In particular, the academic community is charged with acting as 'the critic and conscience of society'. As Grant Duncan of Massey University points out, academics must *exercise* academic freedom (and one might add, fight fiercely to retain the safeguard). Other related sectors include the media of different kinds, unions, NGOs, activist groups, faith-based institutions. We vitally need an aroused and responsive populace that works supportively together to identify and dispute the practices identified here. Imagine (bizarrely) the drive that animates rugby in New Zealand directed to combating the so-called 'free market'.

The second step is to propose valid and responsible alternatives. It is an engaging prospect to describe principles and features of a society that would promote maximum wellbeing for the bulk of the population. One can expect that any such attempt would be instantly dismissed or ridiculed by the existing power structures. We should therefore remember what Gandhi said: "First they ignore you. Then they laugh at you. Then they fight you. Then you win."

The third step is to put alternatives into action. Very often the best way of doing so is in small work units, with limited goals, carefully detailed steps and active solidarity.

Here's an illustration based on tertiary institutions in New Zealand. With minimal change, it might equally apply to government ministries, municipal government, service agencies, public-service institutions and, reasonably enough, businesses and industry.

Tertiaries in New Zealand display a strongly top-down structure of management, with firmly established systems of control, accountability and monitoring. Long gone are the days of trust. But other times and other places have built powerfully on *collegiality*, which is a way of describing mutual support and trust. Tertiaries could easily revert to supportive systems of colleagues working together cooperatively to advance the goals of the institution, rather than inspect, assess and rate individual performance, as applies at present. Academic institutions thrive on mutual support and open sharing of knowledge. (So, one might add, do many other types of institutions.) A goal of the collegial tertiary institution should be to foster and promote a maximum of collaborative interaction through its practices, structures, committees and, above all, outlook. My reading of current tertiaries is that outside the managerial frames set up in the institutions, teachers readily cooperate in their academic lives of teaching, research, publishing and curriculum development. But such sharing is a residual culture of generous support that persists despite the punitive, judgemental processes of present-day performance and institutional management. (I recall a dean of research once effortlessly explaining a "system of carrot and stick" to encourage staff to reach research goals that would enhance the institution's research profile. He never once mentioned a collegial research culture.)

This would require an act of will, but a determined department could set out to reorient its own practice in favour of collegiality as an explicit and comprehensive policy. The challenge would be to persist with its policies in the face of management disapproval, putting its faith and trust in the shared contribution of fellow staff, while evolving responsible principles of proceeding. (I should add that I worked in just such a department for 30 years in Canada.)

An alternative: Fairness as the bottom line

Looking hard at free-market practices prompts one to think of principles that could guide a much more just society. The exercise is not to match free-market inequities with opposing pointers, but to identify basic notions of fairness and social justice. Here's a short list.

An over-riding principle is to *identify* and then *defend the public good*. In New Zealand the idea has been so systematically undermined over the last three decades that it scarcely has any traction left. But it is a powerful base-line for the overall wellbeing of a nation, in many senses. Mostly, supporters of free markets simply ignore the notion. Would they actually argue against it?

An obviously related value is *democratic practice*. An obviously predictable response is, "You've already got it. Vote in the next election." But as one commentator said rather witheringly some years ago, "Some people think there's a connection between the idea of democracy and dropping a piece of paper into a ballot box." The question is, who gets listened to? In the period of the 1980s' social reforms, hundreds of thousands of Kiwis took to the streets in protest. The reforms went ahead regardless. Certainly we need to vote. But we also need to insist on genuine democratic practice into the bargain, and that involves structures for listening to the populace as a way of evolving principled decisions that serve the public good.

Such listening calls for genuine *consultation* of the people and informed groups. The John Key Government of recent years has been notoriously cavalier in treating consultation as a meaningless charade, and blandly asserting its comforting mantra of "a balanced approach". At the same time, however, it is very good at listening to its wealthy backers in order to carry out their agenda. The thrust of this book is that we need a sharply different agenda to serve the best interests of the collective bulk of the population.

A very powerful notion of *collective care* helped usher in welfare state provisions in various countries following the Great Depression. One vital outcome was single-payer national health-care systems, which have transformed the health of nations. It is notable that the privatised health and insurance system of the United States devotes more energy to attacking and distorting the universal health care north of its border than to learning from it. But within Canada, despite serious moves to undermine and privatise healthcare in the country, its original notion of an institutionally 'caring society' still holds. It is highly prized by the population.

A universal health-care system is a means of *sharing resources*. As such, it's a principle worth extending across the needs of a nation, in particular around the necessities of life. Water is an obvious resource. It is essential to life and therefore odious that leaders like Margaret Thatcher saw fit to privatise it, with disastrous results. Unfortunately, New Zealand's National-led government is keenly determined to promote activities that drain and imperil water supplies in the country. Three cases illustrate the point. Across the country, government is strongly encouraging dairying, but without adequate mitigating effects, in an activity that demands high use of water, while creating massive damage to land and water from nitrogen and phosphorus. In Canterbury, the government sacked the elected regional council in order to undemocratically institute its own agency to distribute water to private dairy interests. And in Hawke's Bay, government fully supports the massively suspect Ruataniwha Dam project. In all these cases, it's possible to give a specious and distorting defence of the practice, but only if one is willing to accept the argument for special-interest groups at the expense of the rest of the population.

A similar situation exists in the marine environment with regard to aquaculture, or fish-farming. In 2011 the government passed the Aquaculture Legislation Amendment Bill (No 3) which removed the requirement for Aquaculture Management Areas to be established before consent applications could be made. The resulting simplification of the consent process was welcomed by the industry, which is keen to extend salmon farms and to set up kingfish farms in sensitive areas such as the Firth of Thames.

Getting to the heart of such issues calls for *transparency and honesty*. They are in dramatically short supply in New Zealand's international 'trade' negotiations, most notably the TPPA. The relevant minister, Tim Groser, simply dismisses any hint of public disclosure – "You don't negotiate in public." But the effect is that New Zealanders are being asked to take on faith an astoundingly dubious process and proposal, with clear signs that it will disadvantage Kiwis. Yet we'll need to wait till four years after the agreement is signed before the secret text will be revealed to a deliberately uninformed population.

Transparency implies *public oversight* of public funds. This notion should be entirely familiar to free marketers: they love accountability. It's just that they insist on applying it to *others* – employees, teachers, beneficiaries, for instance. Granted, there is a segment of society that complains loudly that "taxation is theft". But we need to affirm that taxation is revenue – income for a responsible government to spend in the interests of its populace. Such a level of trust would be much easier to develop if it could be publicly evident where funding has gone. There are, after all, many ways of covering up, misrepresenting and concealing accounts.

The public good would be served by squarely confronting the need for *regulation* in society. Massive de-regulation in New Zealand has brought us death in our mines and forests, leaky homes, industrial pollution and much more. It's high time we came of age, dropped the phoney life of self-regulation, and made values of safety and conservation priorities for the wellbeing of the nation.

To conclude, a word on words. The free-market language identified in an earlier chapter has succeeded in swamping a great deal of public discussion, in and beyond economics. To bring about a fairer kind of society, we need unapologetically to promote a different language, perhaps building on some of the terms in this chapter, and starting with *the public good*. This will not be an easy task. The kind of world-view carefully constructed in the last few decades is deliberately one of hard-boiled economics – it's a tough world, competition is fierce, only the resolute survive. Given the conditions that brought on the Global Financial Crisis, there's a perverse logic there. Greed created collapse, yet it wasn't the private sector that saved itself. It was public finance, so we don't need to have a guilty conscience in going in to bat for the public good.

An enlightened world would talk enthusiastically about social justice, fairness, a caring society, integrity, equity, the welfare of citizens, cooperation. A society built around such concepts would be far more just than anything the free market has created.

Kiwi Know Thyself

Dylan Horrocks

"KNOW THYSELF" HE SAYS...
BUT HOW?
HEY! LET ME HELP!
ME ME
ASK ME ANYTHING!
YUP YUP YUP
OKAY- WHO AM I *REALLY*? WHAT AM I LIKE?
OH THAT'S EASY!
YOU'RE GOOD AT SPORTS!
YOU'RE CLEAN & GREEN!
YOU'RE HIP TO TH' GROOVE!
YUP YUP
THAT'S IT?
WHADDAYA WANT? ANALYSIS?
THIS IS THE ENTERTAINMENT BIZNESS CHUMP!
YOU WANT LOCAL CONTENT, GO BUG THE GOLDFISH!
THIS IS GETTING ME NOWHERE!
I'LL GO ASK MY MATES DOWN AT THE MARKET.
MIGHT BE ABLE TO FLOG OFF SOME WOOL WHILE I'M AT IT...
NZ WOOL
SOON...
...SO WHAT AM I LIKE, GUYS? *REALLY*?
NZ WOOL
YOU'RE SMALL.
YOU'RE STUPID.
YOU TALK FUNNY.
NO ONE TAKES YOU SERIOUSLY.
€
OH. WELL... UH...
...WHO WOULD LIKE SOME FINE WOOL?
NZ WOOL
LOOK! TAIWAN'S GOT CHEAP COMPUTER PARTS!!
WHERE?!
QUIT SHOVIN!
OUT OF MY WAY!
ME FIRST!
WOO WOO!

LATER...
MAYBE THEY'RE RIGHT. THEY'RE SO MUCH BIGGER AND LOUDER AND MORE EXCITING THAN I COULD EVER BE...
I SHOULD JUST SHUT UP AND DO WHAT-EVER THEY TELL ME TO...
DON'T LISTEN TO THOSE BULLIES!
THEY JUST WANT TO EXPLOIT YOU!
YOU DON'T NEED 'EM - YOU CAN GO YOUR OWN WAY!
JUST BE YOUR-SELF!
CHILLY
"BE YOURSELF."
Sigh
BUT WHAT IF THEY WON'T LET ME?
I KNOW WHAT YOU MEAN, SIGNOR.
I USED TO BE MYSELF. BUT THEN I WAS GENETICALLY MODIFIED TO TURN ME INTO A FLYING SOYA BEAN.
NOW I HAVEN'T THE FAINTEST IDEA WHO I AM...
WHO AM I?
WHAT AM I DOING HERE?
WHERE AM I GOING?
WHAT DO I WANT FROM LIFE?
MORE PORK!
Sigh! I SHOULD'VE JUST TOLD HIM TO DITCH THE QUEEN AND COME UP WITH A NEW FLAG...
- DYLAN HORROCKS - 99

The Wider View

Let's Make a Deal: The TPPA

Jane Kelsey

The Trans-Pacific Partnership Agreement (TPPA) is billed as a treaty to promote and facilitate free trade between the 12 countries currently involved in negotiations. In this interview-based article Jane Kelsey dispels that claim.

The nature of the TPPA

There are three ways of looking at the TPPA. One, it's a *geo-political device,* led by the US to re-secure its presence as a global power, in an economic and foreign policy sense, especially as a counter to the growing power of China.

Then there are *commercial interests* that shape the nature of this generation of agreements. They are described as 21st century rules that go further behind the border in setting disciplines on governments than any previous agreements have. That means the TPPA is not about trade and certainly not free trade. It's about setting rules that are designed by and for the largest corporate interests. They want to move beyond old-fashioned commodity trade across borders to promote their trans-national operations – movement of money, data, services and commodities – in the most unrestricted way possible. But it's also regulated to serve the interests of the major players who can dominate those markets. There are very few players in New Zealand that could take significant advantage of the model.

The third layer is *power politics* – an agreement of 12 unequal states. Now the play is between the US and Japan, sometimes in tandem, and sometimes in antagonism. The current reason why the agreement has not been concluded is that Japan and the US are 'elephants' fighting in a room. As soon as that is resolved, there will be enormous pressure to close the deal. So the notion that New Zealand is an equal player in that process is an illusion (even to pursue the interests of our mega corporations, which are very few and predominantly Fonterra).

I mentioned regulation. One of the fictions of market economics is that it's about deregulation. In fact it's about making sure regulation serves capital, creating a hybrid of public and private power. So the state – in this case the government – is the agent of a process that enables capital to define the rules, benefit from the rules and in many cases, implement and police the rules.

That's basically what these agreements are about, ever since the North American Free Trade Agreement (NAFTA). Since

1994, the World Trade Organisation has expanded the rules on intellectual property monopoly rights to make new sets of rules to benefit international capital and especially finance capital. The chapters in these 'trade' agreements have continued to expand. One of the most controversial is the inclusion of investment chapters, as in the TPPA, which have put major restrictions on governments imposing new regulations and policy. Foreign investors can enforce their special privileges by bringing cases against states in offshore tribunals rather than domestic courts.

We've started to see more rules restricting areas such as food safety standards, competition policy, controls over the finance sector. The TPPA has around 29 chapters, although they won't tell us what they are. The vast majority are about regulatory restraints on *government* and aside from the leaks, the detail remains secret. One leaked chapter on regulatory coherence tries to lock in the kind of light-handed approach to regulation that brought us Pike River and leaky buildings. And that's been promoted by New Zealand, Australia and the US. There's a chapter on transparency, which is about the need to ensure affected *commercial interests* have input into the policy-making process. So it's not just the substance of regulation that's being disciplined; it's the process of regulating and who has priority rights in taking part.

There are echoes here of the MAI – the Multilateral Agreement on Investment – which itself drew heavily on NAFTA. The anti-MAI campaigns made them controversial, as have some leaks of the TPPA text. Some countries have begun to back off agreements of this kind, partly because of some outrageous cases such as the Philip Morris case against Australia on plain tobacco packaging. And some countries, led in particular by South Africa, are now seeking different models of investor protection that don't follow this track. So the US is desperately trying to lock in as many countries as possible through the TPPA model. New Zealand seems to be falling into line.

Effects of the TPPA

Probably the earliest effect of the TPPA will be on the availability of medicines under Pharmac. People won't have to pay more for prescriptions, but more of the health boards' medicine budget will go to the pharmaceutical companies, with the result that they can then afford to subsidise fewer medicines. Another early impact is likely to be on people's use of the internet – making ISP providers become copyright police, even blocking websites, and possibly imposing criminal penalties on users.

The bigger impacts will be the constraints on governments' ability to address problems. For instance, Labour wants to introduce policies like the Kiwi Assure insurance option. There's pressure to re-regulate the mining sector and ban fracking, and talk about restrictions on hot money flows. All of those would be subject to the rules themselves and to threats of investor-state disputes. It could be much harder to push progressive moves such as promoting organics and restricting GE.

Most worrying are the constraints on government during a major economic or financial crisis. The existing US agreement has absolutely reckless constraints on governments restricting capital movements. New Zealand is vulnerable because we have a very high level of external debt here and households are so deeply indebted that we will need to have the maximum regulatory flexibility to be able to pre-empt or respond to crises. But we will have signed that away.

Enforcing the agreement

There are various ways of enforcing the agreement. Most of the chapters have surveillance mechanisms, where the different countries can oversee each other's compliance with the rules. They will set up various committee structures to conduct surveillance and to demand answers and explanations. It can turn into a harassment mechanism to intimidate governments from taking independent action or from changing things in ways that other governments don't like. Although the national level officials dealing with the policies won't know anything about the agreements or the rules, they will be expected to comply with them and potentially divert a whole lot of resources into responding to these questions. If the other state isn't satisfied, it can move on to the next phase of formal consultations. After that, the other government, and in many cases their investors, could launch a dispute before an ad hoc tribunal, which isn't governed by the normal kind of rules or precedents that operate in our domestic courts. In most instances, the judges will not be people with expertise in the subject area – they'll be trade, investment and diplomatic officials.

It's less of a problem with states because they tend to be quite reluctant to bring disputes against each other, partly for diplomatic reasons and partly because they all tend to not comply on certain things. When it comes to investors though, they don't have those diplomatic constraints. They are governed by commercial self-interest, so they are the most likely to use the enforcement powers, especially to have a chilling effect on government. It's the threat of a dispute: if you don't back off this, we'll sue you.

That's what they tried to do with tobacco, and with fracking in Canada. Then if it goes to a dispute, it can get prolonged. It's extremely costly, an average of around US$8m, sometimes up to $40–50m. That's largely done in secret, with very few rules. There are arbitrators who are also litigators, so they have a potential conflict of interest to provide interpretations and outcomes that are good for their business. We expect some cosmetic changes designed to defuse these criticisms – it's an attempt to re-legitimise a highly discredited process.

Enforcement is the hard end of the spectrum. One TPPA state can't force another to abandon a measure that's been found to breach the TPPA, because parliamentary sovereignty still applies. They cannot unilaterally remake our laws from outside the country. But only the big players can really say no. If it is a really important domestic measure, a government might dig its toes in. The US constantly breaches these agreements because there's a political constituency that's more important than being seen to break the rules and cop the penalty. A country like New Zealand views itself as an exemplary citizen on compliance. We, and Australia, think it's a blight on our reputation to be subject to a dispute. So our govermnents are likely to buckle.

The problem is much bigger with investment disputes, which could happen if a new government sought to re-nationalise the privatised assets or force the renegotiation of PPP contracts. If New Zealand lost in an investor–state tribunal, the tribunal cannot force the government to change the law. But they could impose a massive financial penalty on the government, not just for the immediate losses, but for future lost profits from those changes, and compound interest on the losses. Some of the recent examples have been outrageous. So you're talking not just hundreds of millions, but in some cases billions of dollars. It's a pretty significant lever.

Who's in the tent

It would be good to know what the government is doing and saying in the negotiations, but we don't because it's secret. All of the preparatory documents remain secret until four years after the agreement comes into force. By that time of course, the government that did it would be out of power and unaccountable. That's why the leaks have been particularly useful, especially the ones that have shown country positions, because that reveals what shifts have been happening. The New Zealand process has been amongst the least open, less even than countries which are criticised for being undemocratic, such as Malaysia.

The US has a mechanism for consultation, with a variety of trade advisory groups, almost all of whom represent corporate interests. Some get to see the texts, in some cases they claim to have helped write them. Members of Congress have now forced the administration to allow them to see the draft text or excerpts of it, but in a closed room with no pen and paper and no advisors. They can't tell anyone once they've seen it.

In New Zealand, the opposition, even the friendly opposition, have not been allowed to see the text. So the government's line is 'trust us'. Now, it's clear that the current National-led government supports private interests, with minimal public-interest regulations. So we can expect that their notion of the national interest will reflect the commercial interest of major New Zealand players, principally Fonterra.

Tim Groser has admitted that if people knew what was going on, they probably wouldn't be able to reach an agreement. That's why it's secret. If it was a domestic process, we would never accept this kind of entrenched enforceable legislation being made in secret by the executive, bypassing parliament. It is outrageous that government expects it to be acceptable, because it happens to be under the rubric of an international treaty.

On its side, the US has its own complications. The US Constitution gives Congress power over trade, which creates a problem, because Congress could then unpick a final agreement.

The way around that is a process called *fast-track*, now rebranded as the Trade Promotion Authority. The Administration is moving in Congress to get it, but there is huge opposition there. John Key conceded the US may not get fast-track and, in fact, Congress may not approve the agreement at all. But then he goes on to say we need to get it finished as soon as possible. That means that our government is prepared to sign an agreement making concessions that Obama can't guarantee to deliver on. It's reckless in the extreme.

Stopping the TPPA

Several things could stop the TPPA coming to fruition. For one, if the US and Japan do not agree on agriculture and automobiles, the US will not make any concessions to New Zealand on dairy. The US thinks it can only sell such a deal to its domestic constituency if they have access into Japan's market as compensation. And there is a huge resistance inside Japan.

Another obstacle would be a major leak of the text before it's signed. That would show that it is a shonky deal, and domestic political pressure could make it impossible for governments to proceed to formal signing.

Third, some countries could drop out. Chile, for example, has said that it wants some things re-negotiated and it doesn't like the deal.

And for a fourth, it could be agreed to, but *not ratified*, in various countries. An agreement only comes into force in a country if it goes through its formal constitutional processes for adopting a treaty. It's possible there could be sufficient political backlash for ratification not to occur. And it could be that some countries that are at the table for foreign policy reasons may just never ratify it.

There's also the question of how on earth they're going to make a readable, workable text out of a shambles. The leaks showed massive disagreement about the environment text, the intellectual property chapter, the medicines transparency chapter annex. The state-owned enterprise chapter has been a total dog's breakfast – it's a legal nightmare.

But ultimately we must remember that this is a political deal and that it has its own dynamic.

Climate Change

Ruth Irwin

In the entire history of humanity, civilisation has never coped with such a deep-seated and global problem as climate change. There are many complex reasons for this. Its effects are global but we have no global governance, only global legislative guidance through the UN. *All* countries with industrial pollutants affect the entire planet and thus *all* need to modify their behaviour. Scientific evidence on this scale has never been gathered before.

Climate change has been made worse by free-market practices, which are based on the mistaken belief that rational people act in their own self-interest. Markets traditionally are justified for fairly redistributing scarcity, not limiting permission to pollute. Policy makers assume that the best way to modify modern corporate and individual behaviour is exclusively economic. Infrastructure is 'hard wired' and difficult to modify in a short time period. Modernity has normalised selfish individualism and the immediate satisfaction of desires and pays little attention to the wellbeing of ecological systems of the entire planet. Modern philosophy prioritises the human mind over the rest of ecology and fails to understand how interconnected we all are.

Greenhouse effect

Climate change is the shift in mean temperature across the whole planet. As humanity has developed modern industrial technology, we have released vast quantities of pollutants: coal smoke, oil, diesel, bitumen, and other chemical cocktails, into the atmosphere. The planet has warmed up dramatically over the last 100 years (see Intergovernmental Panel on Climate Change for the science).

The greenhouse effect is a result of sunlight being absorbed rather than reflecting, as much as it used to, out into space. We have thickened up the atmosphere with dirty particles. Certain chemicals have the ability to 'capture' sunlight as it comes into the atmosphere. Instead of hitting a shiny surface like water or snow, the light hits a particle and heats it up. The energy is captured as the particle increases its intensity. This is the greenhouse effect. Only chemicals that resonate in the infrared spectrum create the greenhouse effect. They include methane, sulphur dioxide and carbon dioxide, and a few others. Collectively they are known as 'carbon dioxide equivalents', or CO_2e.

We have solved this problem once before. In the 1990s the ozone hole became very pronounced and scientists realised it was created by the gas, hydrochlorofluorocarbon (HCFC) – a key ingredient in refrigerators. After some controversy, HCFC was banned worldwide. Immediately the ozone hole began to improve, although it still exists and remains a problem decades later. The gases often take a long period to filter into the upper atmosphere and wreak their havoc. CO_2 has a 30-year lag, so the greenhouse effect we see now is from pollution that was released 30 years ago.

The key to solving the climate change crisis is to stop all greenhouse gases from being released into the atmosphere. Unfortunately not all of them are still under human control. As the atmosphere has warmed up, natural feedbacks are beginning to occur. For a long time, the ocean absorbed CO_2 but beginning in 2005, the ocean has now heated so much that in the northern hemisphere's summer (which is hotter than the southern hemisphere) the ocean actually releases CO_2 instead of absorbing it. Even worse, in Siberia, permafrost is melting after thousands of years of freezing the underlying tundra. The melting substrata is peaty soil, now rotting down and releasing millions of tonnes of methane – one of the worst of the greenhouse gases. So our only hope – and it is definitely viable – is to halt all CO_2e pollution as quickly as possible in the hope that we can reverse the feedbacks before we have 'runaway climate change'.

Political solutions

The best way to avoid runaway climate change is through immediate regulation. Individual nations can put legislation in place, but the problem is a global one. One solution is a United Nations Climate Accord, in similar fashion to the Ozone Accord.

There are three main problems to an immediate regulatory halt to greenhouse gases. (Ozone gases were phased out over some five years.) Modern cities were built during the petroleum boom and are spread out, poor in public transport, and difficult to live in if you only have bicycles or walking. So infrastructure and city design are real obstacles to abruptly reducing fossil fuels. Furthermore, the oil lobby is immensely powerful and has had a huge impact on creating scepticism about the truth of climate change. This has slowed down the political will to regulate. The final problem is that many university researchers and policy makers exist in a worldview that assumes economics and technological innovation are the main levers for effecting change. This neoliberal worldview has profoundly limited the available solutions.

Global climate change has been exclusively framed in scientific or economic terms, with a passing reference to historical responsibility from more 'developed' nations, and present responsibility for future generations. Every year the UN holds a Global Climate Change meeting in December, but since the meeting in Kyoto in 1992 we have not even been able to establish binding commitments to reduce greenhouse emissions. Largely this is because all the policy directions to reduce CO_2e are aimed at economic behaviouralism, despite all the evidence that economic 'choice' is not making any difference at all. In New Zealand, a neoliberal Emissions Trading Scheme (ETS) began in 2008, and was successively watered down in 2009 and 2012. The ETS is a market, like all neoliberal markets. Instead of making political decisions in a governmental setting, the belief is that the neoliberal market will depoliticise all decisions, and replace self-interested lobbying with the Invisible Hand's market equilibrium.

Really effective solutions are not merely economic. They include changes in city design, infrastructure, public transport, renewable power, house insulation, low food miles, and better agricultural practice. They also require a lot of investment in new technologies and new ways of caring for the planet and each other. Alternative economic measures include carbon tax, which is regulated by government and offers clear price signals to all sectors of the economy. A tax is also redistributive and encourages equality instead of a steady transfer of money from the poor to the rich.

For the last 25 years the United Nations has been trying to manage this global problem with central legislation and binding commitments such as the Kyoto Protocol. 196 nations eventually signed Kyoto. Historically, richer, more 'developed' nations have released greenhouse gases for much longer and in much larger quantities than poorer, less 'developed' nations. Thus, Kyoto has two tiers to its agreement. Developed nations agreed to reduce their greenhouse gas emissions (CO_2e) 20% below 1990 levels by 2020. That gave 30 years for improvements in knowledge, technology, and infrastructure to improve the rate of CO_2e emissions. The UN made a case for economic behavioural policies to be put in place to encourage people in nation states to change their ways and emit less CO_2e.

New Zealand was one of the first countries to sign the binding commitment to Kyoto. But then we put the problem into the politically 'too hard' basket, and did very little to implement a reduction in emissions for decades. Helen Clark created a Climate Change Commission in 2002. However, it was not until the end of the fourth Labour Government's nine years in power that Helen Clark introduced an Emissions Trading Scheme which aimed to make all sectors of the economy account and pay for their climate emissions.

As an economic and policy solution, the Emissions Trading Scheme (ETS) was encouraged through many UN legislative measures, beginning with the Brundtland Report in 1988. Brundtland recommended an early version of 'Third Way' economics. In other words, she modified the strictly consumer-oriented rationality of market 'choice' (see earlier chapter on neoliberal theory) with the aims of 'sustainability'. Traditional neoliberal market theory believes that there are no political decisions but rather the Invisible Hand smooths out the costs for producers and the benefits for consumers and results in a 'balanced' price. There are lots of factors that are 'externalities' and are not accounted in the profit calculations of cost–benefit. Pollution of all kinds often consists of 'externalities' that are borne by the environment and the public, rather than the companies that produce the pollution or the consumers that benefit from the manufacture of goods and services. Brundtland expanded what needs to be accounted in the cost–benefit model to include environmental pollution and degradation. She also included the needs of future generations into the market equation. Sustainability still relies heavily on the assumptions of market rationality; it simply expands the accountability of the cost–benefit exercise to include environmental impacts and future generations. The assumption is that the market will encourage efficiencies and innovation, so pricing carbon emissions will encourage a reduction in emissions.

Following the Brundtland Report, the UN encouraged Emissions Trading Schemes (ETS) as a global solution to climate change. The aim was to set a price on emissions to make it much more expensive to emit greenhouse-gas pollution. The rationale for a market in emissions is that markets encourage technological innovation and efficiency and some forms of pollution are easier to limit than others. If it is extremely difficult to reduce emissions, then industries will have to buy permits to emit, whereas if the industry is capable of easily and cheaply reducing the amount they emit, they can 'sell' the amount they have saved. Initially the concept of the emissions trading market was to limit or 'cap' the amount of permits available, and gradually reduce them over time so that pressure to continue to create cleaner technology gets continuously implemented.

Like all neoliberal markets, the ETS was originally designed to impact on an individual's decision-making. This is part of the justification for privatising electricity-generating companies, so that individual consumers can 'choose' cleaner (and/or cheaper) energy between providers. But consumer choice has made little impact on electricity generators so this argument has largely dropped out of the ETS rhetoric. Instead, the ETS evolved into a trade between large-scale corporate emitters.

New Zealand and the Kyoto Protocol

The Kyoto Protocol committed us to reducing emissions 20% below 1990 levels by the year 2020. We produced about 60 gigatonnes (Gg) of CO_2e in 1990. According to government statistics, by 2011, our emissions had risen by 22% to 72 Gg CO_2e. We are now more than 20% *above* 1990 levels – requiring us to slow our emissions by some 40% to reach our Kyoto obligations by 2020.

We signed the Kyoto Protocol expecting to easily stay within our emissions obligations because of our huge forestry which 'absorbs' CO_2e. However, in the lead up to beginning the New Zealand ETS, vast quantities of forest were felled and the land sold to dairy farmers. This was done in anticipation of the high cost of taking land out of forestry production once the ETS was in commission. Under the ETS, forestry includes the profit of ETS carbon units, but if the forest is felled and not replaced, those carbon units have to be paid out by the owner. To avoid that burden, mass forestry was transferred to pasture and New Zealand went from a gross absorber to a gross emitter of CO_2e. To demonstrate this with figures, in 1990, New Zealand's *net* emissions – which is the amount we emit minus the amount forests absorb – was 31,530.4 Gg CO_2e. By 2011 our net emissions had gone up by 88% to 59,294.7 Gg CO_2e. That is an astronomical increase in overall emissions, which gives New Zealand the dubious distinction of being one of the worst countries, per capita, in the world.

Furthermore, Federated Farmers and Fonterra have been powerful lobby groups, managing to successfully argue that reducing CO_2e in the agricultural sector is nearly impossible. They launched a scathing attack on the 'fart tax' in 2003, which argued that stopping cows and sheep from belching carbon dioxide was not possible without reducing stock numbers, and thus attacking one of our staples of the New Zealand economy. Agriculture has successfully lobbied to remain outside the ETS ever since.

Since then it has become better understood that there are a lot of changes that can be made to farming practices that will successfully reduce the CO_2e emissions of each beast and the need for so many 'units' of stock. Nitrogen fertiliser top-dressing for example, increases the amount of nitrous oxide emissions and better forms of pasture management reduce these requirements considerably. At the moment, the singular reliance on the ETS to create change means there is no regulation, nor any other (dis)incentive to farmers to alter their fertiliser, their pasture management, the number of trees and diversity on their land, or their stock numbers. Given that agriculture is responsible for roughly half New Zealand's greenhouse gas emissions, this is a huge hole in the governance of our emissions profile.

Changing the mindset

The ETS has been a miserable failure worldwide. Russia flooded the market with emissions permits, so the price dropped to less than $2.75/unit in 2013. New Zealand's ETS has New Zealand units, most of which are freely allocated to various industries. If a company needs more, they can buy more on the global ETS market or pay the government $25 per unit. The low price of global permits makes financial incentives to innovate a farce. Both the National and Labour parties are committed to the ETS scheme.

The alternative within the economic framework is an Emissions Tax. Finland, Sweden, Ireland, British Columbia and Australia are examples of successful Carbon Tax schemes. British Columbia started at $10 per ton and then increased by $5 per year until it hit $30 per ton of emissions. The tax is 'revenue neutral', which means, unlike the ETS which aims to profit companies and traders, the tax revenue is redeployed to help companies with research, development and capital costs to further reduce emissions, with public infrastructure such as public transport, or as a personal tax rebate. In all the places the Carbon Tax has been introduced it has been remarkably effective at reducing emissions.

Most people would like to reduce their carbon footprint. The most obvious impediment to achieving this is the lack of infrastructure which would make it not only possible, but easy, to live a low-carbon life: better, denser city design, regulations on well-insulated, carbon-neutral building, frequent and efficient public transport, cycleways, renewable energy, better forestry and agricultural processes, and soft mitigation to problems such as sea-level rise are all part of the solution. While there are no single or short-term answers, individual actions can only make a small impact on the problem. Climate change is large scale and needs to be leveraged at the local, national and global government, and corporate levels.

For corporations and governments to make the required changes, we all need a deep shift in the normal relationship between people and nature. UNESCO would like to make a Universal Declaration on Climate Change, but political pressure prevents it. Having started in 1988, the Intergovernmental Panel on Climate Change (IPCC) finally introduced a Working Group on Climate Ethics in the latest Report (2013). So far, the IPCC tends to make the same assumptions about economic (dis)incentives as the rest of the UN. Far-reaching, real change needs a shift in mindset, away from privileging human rationality over and above our ecosystems and always focusing on short-term profit. For humanity to thrive, we need to change our thinking towards the long-term. This requires deep understanding of how integrated the human community is with other life forms on our unique planet. We *are* nature. To truly address the ravages of climate change, we need to live *with* nature, not 'use' it. The change in mindset is not just ethically desirable. Our survival is staked on it.

A View from Afar

Jim Stanford

New Zealand's world-famous tourist promotions invariably advertise the country as a land of startling, wonderful contrasts: from mountain-top to surf beach, sub-tropics to tundra, pastoral to urban. So I suppose it's not surprising that New Zealand's political-economy should reflect the same confusing extremes.

Compared to other industrial economies, New Zealand is a small, remote society, relatively cohesive and tightly knit. Perhaps that helps to explain the relatively extreme shifts in economy, politics, and culture that have constantly reshaped Aotearoa over the last generation – for better or (more often) for worse. In larger, more diverse countries, society could not change so dramatically and so quickly.

Some of these sudden changes and experiments were positive. Progressives around the world have been inspired by many New Zealand achievements: the nuclear weapons-free zone declaration and other expressions of global independence; important reforms in democracy and voting systems; the unique recognition given to indigenous political rights. Yet no sooner would we celebrate a hopeful sign from this curious distant land, than we'd be appalled and angered by news of another episode of market-worshipping Kiwi social engineering.

It is hard for foreign observers to reconcile these seemingly contradictory trends. Most puzzling of all, these sudden policy lurches have borne little predictable relationship to which party is in power.

In particular, 'Rogernomics' betrayed basic progressive values under Labour in the mid-1980s – and this was a timely warning to other countries that global social democracy was changing. It also signalled that core principles of social progress were now in great danger – no matter who was in government.

More recently, however, it's been clear who the main enemy is: unapologetic conservatives in the National Party and their allies in the business and investment communities, who continue to push their corporate agenda to new extremes.

There is much to lament about the negative economic, social, and cultural shifts which have been caused here by 30 years of extreme free-market economics. These changes reflect a deliberate effort by those with wealth and power (both here and globally) to reinforce their privilege, to suppress opposition, to reduce expectations, and to construct an ideological world in which there seems to be "no alternative" (as phrased famously by Margaret Thatcher). The other chapters of this book describe well the punishing human and social effects of this agenda, and the way private profit is now valued above human and environmental needs.

On the other hand, for those who aim to build something better, it is also important to take stock of the country's strengths, as well as its weaknesses. It would be easy for Kiwis to feel demoralised by the painful, lopsided, and often wasteful measures that corporations and corporate-friendly politicians have put in place here. New Zealand's physical and cultural distance from other industrial countries might add to feelings of isolation and powerlessness.

Remember, however, that the same struggle over the future shape of society that has been waged by progressive Kiwis, also carries on elsewhere. And corporations don't win all of the battles. Moreover, features of society which may help explain how the corporate agenda was implemented so quickly and extremely in New Zealand – in a small, remote and cohesive society – could also support a future turn-around in direction.[1]

Without being romantic about it, Kiwi culture continues to reflect lasting, positive traits of national independence, collective self-reliance, voluntarism, participation, and respect for community. Those strengths are still clear to an outside observer, regardless of the sad and costly side-effects of three decades of free-market experimentation. I think those features explain why New Zealand workers, families, and communities have managed to survive the challenges of 'reform' as well as they have. And those same traits will be important in building the foundation for a different, more hopeful, and more equal Aotearoa.

New Zealand in international context

This confusing jumble of progressive and backward features becomes plain when we consider New Zealand's experience in international context. Table 1 summarises several measures of economic and social wellbeing. In each case, we compare New Zealand's performance in recent decades to the experience of other advanced capitalist economies (using data from the Organization for Economic Cooperation and Development [OECD]).[2]

New Zealand was once famous not only for one of the highest material standards of living in the world, but also for its early, well-developed welfare state. It had the first old-age pension in the world, the first public housing in the world, and a pioneering system of labour regulation, conciliation, and arbitration that aimed to extend basic democratic rights and the rule of law into the workplace.

All that changed in the late 1970s, as global capital (in both its industrial and its financial forms) began to rebel against the constraints of Keynesian welfare-state capitalism, and against the economic and political gains which labour achieved during the long post-war expansion. A new, tough-love version of capitalist ideology was constructed to radically re-make society through free-market economics. This doctrine, 'neoliberalism', was imposed first under Thatcher and Reagan. It was then enforced internationally through monetary policy, capital flows, globalisation, and ideological imperialism. In New Zealand's case, this sea change was made worse by the shift in external relations resulting from the UK's entry to the European Common Market (and resulting shock to New Zealand's exports), as well as other economic challenges.

The resulting shock to New Zealand's welfare state was among the most dramatic in the developed world. (It is perhaps rivalled now by the equally extreme shock therapy being imposed in Greece and other hard-hit European countries.) The first section of Table 1 describes the major downsizing of New Zealand's government and finances since then. Government tax revenues, and spending on government programmes, both declined more as a share of GDP in New Zealand since the mid-1980s than in any other OECD country.[3] Programme spending (that is, all government spending other than interest payments) fell by almost 10 points of GDP. Half of that drop was eventually reflected in a reduction in taxes (the rest was reflected in the elimination of previous deficits). Indeed, once right-wing governments succeeded in slashing public programmes, they were keen to channel the resulting savings in the form of tax cuts that disproportionately benefited companies and high-income households.

Public debt is very low: net total government debt equaled just 7% of GDP in 2012, down dramatically from the 1980s and 1990s. Budget hawks try to make the fiscal situation look worse than it is: by emphasising gross debt (rather than net debt[4]), for example, or adding up several years of projected future deficits to try to scare Kiwis into accepting still more austerity. But in reality, the government has plenty of financial leeway. Remember, too, that

Table 1: New Zealand in international context: Selected indicators

Variable	Score and Year	Comment
Government		
Total taxes (as % of GDP)	33% (2012), down 5 points since 1986	Biggest reduction in taxes in OECD since 1986.
Programme spending (as % of GDP)	44% (2012), down 10 points since 1986	Biggest reduction in government programme spending in OECD since 1986.
Net public debt (as % of GDP)	78% (2012), down 43 points since 1993	OECD average government debt/GDP ratio *grew* by 30 points in same time.
Labour markets		
Collective bargaining coverage	17% (2010), down 35 points since 1985	5th-lowest bargaining coverage in OECD, and worst deunionisation since 1985.
Employment protections (OECD index)[1]	1.39 (2012)	Among the weakest employment protection laws in OECD.
Minimum wage (as % median wages)	60% (2013)	3rd-highest minimum wage (relative to median earnings) in OECD.
Employment Rate (15–64 yrs, as % pop'n)	72% (2013)	Employment and participation rates still lower than early 1980s.

Variable	**Score and Year**	**Comment**
Economy and trade		
Productivity growth	0.5% (avg. annual growth, 2000–2012)	Ranks 25th of 31 countries, productivity growing one-third as fast as OECD average.
Current account balance (as % of GDP)	–5% (2012)	3rd-worst current account deficit in OECD (after Iceland and Turkey).
GDP per capita	Rank (2012): 21st Rank (1999): 21st	No catch-up to other industrial countries; decline relative to Australia.
Equality, health, environment		
Relative poverty rate (below 50% median inc.)	11% (2008), up 1.2 points since 2000.	Incidence of low income near OECD average, but much worse than 1980s.
Gini coefficient[2]	0.32 (2012), up .055 points since 1982	Biggest increase in inequality in the OECD since mid-1980s.
Life expectancy at birth	81.2 years (2011)	Life expectancy ranks 12th in the OECD.
Infant mortality (per 1000 births)	5.5 (2010), up 0.1 since 1998.	6th-highest infant mortality in OECD, no improvement in last decade.
GHG emissions (tonnes per capita per year)	16.6 (2011)	5th-highest emissions per capita in OECD.

Source: Author's calculations from OECD databases, except for Gini coefficient data (from B. Perry, *Household Income Trends in New Zealand*, Ministry of Social Development, 2014). 1. For regular employees; index scored out of 4. 2. Index of inequality: 0 represents equality, 1 represents full inequality.

public debts have grown rapidly in recent years in most other OECD countries (due to the GFC and resulting recession); this makes New Zealand's very small debt all the more unusual. Far from being a great achievement, however, this radical debt reduction is actually proof of government inaction and irresponsibility. It occurred even as so many vital human and environmental needs were going unmet by government. Reducing the government's financial debt, as the country's social and environmental debts accumulate steadily, is hardly a sign of progress.

The extreme nature of free-market economics is especially visible in New Zealand's labour markets and labour laws. Several relevant indicators are summarised in the second part of Table 1. No country in the entire OECD has experienced more dramatic de-unionisation. Union membership as a share of the workforce fell dramatically (by 35%) in the wake of successive anti-union measures. At present only 17% of New Zealand workers benefit from the protection of a collective agreement – among the lowest of any industrial country.

Statutory labour protections are also extremely weak in New Zealand. For example, the OECD calculates an index of employment protection. New Zealand's score on this measure is among the lowest of any OECD country. Meanwhile, minimum wages are still an effective regulation in this country. Relative to median wages in the overall labour market, the minimum wage floor is stronger than in many other countries. They are still too low, of course, to lift a low-wage worker and their family out of poverty – and minimum wages alone cannot ensure a fair division of wealth across the whole labour market. Maintaining and expanding minimum wages, as well as strengthening other instruments of redistribution (especially collective bargaining), will be key future priorities for those concerned with poverty and inequality in New Zealand.

Has the radical deregulation of New Zealand's labour market fired up employment opportunities, as its advocates promised? Not exactly. As of 2012, some 72% of the prime working-age population (15–64 years old) was in work, placing New Zealand in the mid-range of OECD outcomes. That employment rate was actually still slightly lower than it was in the mid-1980s. In contrast, the employment rate increased in most OECD countries over the same time (driven largely by more women taking paid work). Work is ultimately the source of prosperity, yet fewer New Zealanders are working (relative to population) today than before free-market economics started. That strongly refutes the claim that the painful changes of the past generation were truly necessary to attain an 'efficient' labour market.

Conservatives also claim that getting government "out of the way," strictly controlling public debt, and eliminating inconvenient workplace rules will all unleash the productivity of the private sector. But there's no evidence that this has happened in the wake of New Zealand's financial shock therapy. The third section of Table 1 summarises several indicators of efficiency, output, and trade.

Productivity growth (the amount of value-added produced per hour of labour) has been among the worst of any OECD country. Productivity has grown by just 0.5% per year since the turn of the century (far slower than most countries, and just a fifth of the pace of Korea). This reflects the failure of New Zealand to develop high-technology, innovation-intensive industries (relying instead on traditional resource-based sectors).

And New Zealand has experienced one of the worst trade performances of any OECD country, despite recently enjoying strong prices for many of its exported commodities. The current account deficit (which represents the difference between what a country earns on its exports of goods, services, and incomes, and what it pays for its imports) equaled nearly 5% of GDP in 2012 – third-worst in the OECD. A key factor behind that terrible deficit is the ongoing drain of interest payments and investment income resulting from New Zealand's heavy reliance on foreign direct investment and other forms of foreign debt. That outflow of investment income removes close to $10 billion per year from domestic spending power. It is ironic that right-wing politicians raise such hysteria about a public debt equal to 7% of GDP – yet completely ignore the country's debt to foreign investors, which now equals almost ten times as much (or nearly 70% of GDP).

GDP per capita is commonly used to indicate the general prosperity of an economy (although it can be a misleading benchmark, since it does not take into account income distribution and inequality). By this measure, New Zealand is still a poor cousin within the club of industrial nations. It ranked 21st in 2012 – exactly the same as in 1999. And New Zealand fell still further behind Australia during this period. So it is simply not true to claim that the painful restructuring of New Zealand society over the past 30 years was necessary in order to 'catch up' economically to the rest of the world. It turns out that those painful changes were more aimed at re-dividing the pie, not growing it.

The last section of Table 1 reports several measures of New Zealand's social and environmental performance. Income distribution has become far more uneven under the harsh policies of successive governments. By 2008, relative poverty (the share of Kiwis earning less than half the national median income) had nearly doubled from the early 1980s, to 11%. Poverty in New Zealand is still not the worst in the OECD (and it's much better than the US, at 17%). But it has grown dramatically under free-market policies. Not surprisingly, so has inequality. The 'Gini coefficient' is a way to measure the overall distribution of income.[5] New Zealand's Gini score in fact grew more rapidly since the mid-1980s than in any other OECD country. All of this reflects the negative impact of government downsizing, reduction in income support, and de-unionisation on the division of the economic pie.

Health indicators also reveal that living conditions have stagnated, as a result of large cuts in public and social programmes. Infant mortality is relatively high: 5.5 deaths per 1,000 live births, the sixth-worst in all of the OECD. More worryingly, there has been little improvement in infant mortality for years, despite medical and technical advances. This poor showing likely reflects growing poverty and uneven access to health care (including for Māori families). Life expectancy in New Zealand is in the mid-range of OECD countries, at 81 years.

Finally, despite its nature-friendly reputation, New Zealand continues to rank as one of the worst polluters in the OECD. It pumped out 16.6 tonnes of greenhouse gas emissions per person in 2011, the fifth-worst of any industrial country. New Zealand's focus on resource extraction and industrial agriculture – the centrepiece of the free-market economic plan – means that this poor record will only get worse.

Conclusion: Preserving what's good, building something better

This brief and selective review broadly confirms my earlier impression of New Zealand's troubled and contradictory political-economy. New Zealand was once a world leader in building an economy that was fair, inclusive, and secure. That legacy has been largely, but not totally, undone by 30 years of policies aimed at enhancing private profit and power, rather than enhancing the quality and security of life for most Kiwis. Free-market economics has produced needless suffering, wasted enormous human potential, and devalued social and environmental goals.

Yet despite this pain, New Zealand's performance on job-creation and productivity has been unimpressive at best: not even keeping up with OECD-wide averages, and indeed falling farther behind according to many criteria. This shoots down the claim that hard-nosed market-friendly policies are necessary to spark superior economic performance and prosperity.

However, New Zealand society still retains some important and lasting strengths, visible both in economic and social data, and in popular values and culture. This is true, despite the country having endured some of the most extreme fiscal and labour policies pursued anywhere in the world. Despite their best efforts, those pushing free markets have not succeeded in recreating in Aotearoa the same extremes of inequality and power imbalance that are visible in the US – the role model for global neoliberalism. And there are some policies and structures (such as relatively strong minimum wage laws, and the continuing positive influence of programmes like New Zealand Super and Working for Families) through which New Zealand's previous commitment to equality and inclusion continue to exert positive influence. All this gives progressives a starting point to improve on – one that is far from the worst in the industrialised world.

Most importantly, I would argue that most New Zealanders continue to express deep values that do not fit with free-market ideology. Despite 30 years of one-sided, mean-spirited policy change, New Zealand retains a strong base of 'social capital': respect and trust for each other; willingness to work together; and recognition of the importance of mutual aid for society's survival and prosperity. New Zealanders will not endlessly tolerate inequality and exploitation; right-wing governments are constrained by these popular values and norms.

In sum, I believe this is still ultimately a hopeful place. Workers and communities in New Zealand have an important, proud legacy of striving to build a society that is inclusive, hard-working, and fair. They've shown that great things can be done in a small, remote country. And while the wealthy and privileged in New Zealand rolled back much (but not all) of that progress during the past generation, they do not have the economic or cultural authority to dictate how society evolves. New Zealanders have the power to fundamentally change the direction of this society – and to once again serve as an inspiration for those of us in the rest of the world trying to do the same.

1 Many academic analysts have concluded that a key factor explaining the sustainable welfare state policies of Scandinavia has been the small size and relative cohesiveness of those countries, as well as their (more modest) geographical isolation from the

rest of Europe. Those same factors could potentially work in favour of efforts to rebuild an egalitarian society in New Zealand.

2 Of course, using standardised international data can obscure some of the specific details of New Zealand's performance in each area.

3 For some of the more recent members of the OECD, comparable historical data dating back to the 1980s is not available.

4 Net debt is a better measure of true financial position because it takes into account the value of the government's own financial assets, not just the value of its debt and liabilities.

5 A Gini score of zero represents perfect equality, while 1 represents perfect inequality (where one rich person takes home all the income). A higher score reflects growing inequality.

Contributors

Pat Baskett has an MA in French and is a former feature writer for the *NZ Herald*. Her novel *Beneath a Black Sun* is published as an e-book.

Sue Bradford is a lecturer at Unitec's School of Social Practice in Waitakere, and has just completed a PhD in public policy at AUT. In 1983, she helped set up and sustain the Auckland Unemployed Workers Rights Centre and later the Auckland Peoples Centre. She was a Green Member of Parliament (1999–2009) on welfare and employment issues. Sue is currently co-chair of welfare activist group Auckland Action Against Poverty. Contact: bradford.sue73@gmail.com

Peter Conway was elected CTU Secretary in 2009. Prior, he was CTU Economist and Director of Policy for nine years. He has been active in unions since 1977, when he worked for the Clothing Trades Union. Peter has been assistant national secretary of the New Zealand Distribution Workers Federation, in the National Distribution Union, the Nurses Organisation, and a director of Auckland's Yellow Bus Company.

David Cooke is a Senior Scholar, York University, Toronto, previously Associate-Professor of English and Education at York, and academic staff member of Victoria University of Wellington and Unitec. He worked in language education in China, Cuba, Mozambique, Nicaragua and New Zealand. He is a member of the New Zealand Ethics Committee.

Nesta Devine is Associate Professor in graduate education at Auckland University of Technology. In a former life she was a high school history teacher, and investigated Public Choice Theory to try to understand what was happening to education policy in New Zealand.

Sandra Grey is a Senior Lecturer in Social Policy at Victoria University of Wellington. Sandra is currently working on a major project examining activism by the New Zealand women's, union, and anti-poverty movements since 1970.

Nicky Hager works as an investigative journalist and author. He has written five books about New Zealand politics, intelligence, public relations and military subjects. These include *The Hollow Men*, a study of three years within the New Zealand National Party, and most recently *Other People's Wars*, about New Zealand in Afghanistan and the war on terror.

Kevin Hague is a Member of Parliament for the Green Party of Aotearoa, and prior, worked in health with senior roles in both NGO and government sectors, including as Executive Director of the New Zealand AIDS Foundation and Chief Executive Officer of the West Coast District Health Board. He served on the National Health Committee, and chaired the Public Health Advisory Committee.

Tim Hazledine has been Professor in the Department of Economics at Auckland since 1992. He was raised in Dunedin and went to the Universities of Otago, Canterbury and Warwick. He has taught at these universities and also Balliol College, Oxford, Queen's in Ontario, Canada, and the University of British Columbia in Vancouver. He is interested in competition policy as well as the 'Big Think' issues of inequality and growth.

Mānuka Hēnare (Te Aupōuri; Te Rarawa; Ngāti Kurī) is Associate Professor in Māori Business Development at the University of Auckland Business School and Associate Dean (Māori and Pacific Development). He is also the foundation Director of the Mira Szászy Research Centre for Māori and Pacific Economic Development and leads a number of multidisciplinary research project teams.

Claire Hill is a writer and editor with a BA in Media Studies. She was managing editor and designer of *School's Out!* magazine for six years and has worked on publications such as *Te Rau Mata*, *Speak2Me*, *Go See Discover* and *AA Traveller*.

Dylan Horrocks is a cartoonist, writer and illustrator who lives in Auckland. His cartoons have been published in the *Listener* and the *NZ Political Review* and his books include *Hicksville* and *Incomplete Works*. His website is at hicksvillecomics.com

Ruth Irwin has a PhD in Climate Change Philosophy and Education from the University of Glasgow. She is the author of *Heidegger, Politics and Climate Change* and two edited books, *Climate Change and Philosophy* and *Another Decade of New Zealand Education Policy: Where to Now?* with Martin Thrupp. Contact ruth.irwin@gmail.com.

Mike Joy, M.Sc. (Hons), PhD, is Senior Lecturer in environmental sustainability at the Institute of Agriculture and Environment at Massey University. He is an outspoken advocate for environmental protection in New Zealand and has received a number of awards, including an Ecology in Action award from the New Zealand Ecological Society; an Old Blue award from the Royal Forest and

Bird Protection Society; 2009 Environmental New Zealander of the year by *North and South* magazine; 2012 person of the year by the Manawatu Evening Standard; and 2013 Royal Society Charles Fleming Award for Environmental Achievement.

Helen Kelly has been President of the Council of Trade Unions since 2007. She is a vigorous advocate for women's pay and employment equity through legislative and social change. Helen is deeply committed to highlighting the importance of having safe and healthy workplaces in, for example, the forestry industry.

Jane Kelsey is Professor of Law at the University of Auckland and a long-time critic of New Zealand's neoliberal policies and their counterparts, international free trade and investment agreements. She has actively monitored and fostered debate on the Trans-Pacific Partnership Agreement since the negotiations began in 2010.

John Minto is a political activist, best known for his involvement in the protests against the 1981 Springbok tour of New Zealand. He is co-vice-president of the Mana Movement, a spokesperson for Global Peace and Justice Auckland and a National vice-chairperson of the Quality Public Education Coalition.

Anne-Marie O'Neill has taught graduate and undergraduate courses in the sociology of education, gender, curriculum and policy at Massey University College of Education and published widely in these areas. She is currently completing her doctorate on the politics of 'Governmentality, curriculum and assessment reform in Aotearoa New Zealand'.

John O'Neill is Professor of Teacher Education at Massey University. He is actively involved in public and media debates on state school privatisation, class-size increases, National Standards and quality teaching. His focus is on the way education policy shapes teachers' work and learning, and informal teaching and learning in everyday activities and settings.

Michael A. Peters is Professor of Education at the University of Waikato and Emeritus Professor in Educational Policy, Organisation and Leadership at the University of Illinois at Urbana-Champaign. He is executive editor of the journal *Educational Philosophy and Theory*, and editor of three international e-journals, *Policy Futures in Education*, *E-Learning and Digital Media*, and *Knowledge Cultures*.

Bill Rosenberg is Economist and Director of Policy at the New Zealand Council of Trade Unions (NZCTU) since 2009 and has a PhD in Mathematical Psychology. He publishes on economic and labour issues, globalisation and trade, and "News media ownership in New Zealand". Earlier, Bill worked as Deputy Director, Centre for Teaching and Learning at the University of Canterbury. He was a Commissioner on the board of the Tertiary Education Commission and National President of the Association of University Staff.

Charles Sedgwick is a sociologist with strong interdisciplinary interests. During the course of his career he has taught at the University of Canterbury and at Victoria University of Wellington.

Jim Stanford is an economist with Unifor, Canada's largest private-sector trade union, and author of *Economics for Everyone: A Short Guide to the Economics of Capitalism* (London: Pluto). He has a PhD in economics from the New School for Social Research in New York. He lived in New Zealand for six months in 2010.

The Rt Hon. Sir Edmund Thomas LLB(NZ) LLD(VUW) KNZM QC is a retired Judge of the Court of Appeal and a former Acting Judge of the Supreme Court. He is presently a Distinguished Fellow at the University of Auckland Law School. He authored *The Judicial Process: Realism, Pragmatism, Practical Reasoning and Principles*. In 2013 he gave the Bruce Jesson Lecture entitled 'Reducing Inequality: A Strategy for a Cause'.

Index